Cambridge Student Guide

Shakespeare

Antony and Cleopatra

Rex Gibson

Series Editor:

CAMBRIDGE
UNIVERSITY PRESS

PUBLISHED BY THE PRESS SYNDICATE OF THE UNIVERSITY OF CAMBRIDGE
The Pitt Building, Trumpington Street, Cambridge, United Kingdom

CAMBRIDGE UNIVERSITY PRESS
The Edinburgh Building, Cambridge CB2 2RU, UK
40 West 20th Street, New York, NY 10011–4211, USA
477 Williamstown Road, Port Melbourne, VIC 3207, Australia
Ruiz de Alarcón 13, 28014 Madrid, Spain
Dock House, The Waterfront, Cape Town 8001, South Africa

http://www.cambridge.org

First published 2004

Printed in the United Kingdom at the University Press, Cambridge

Typeface 9.5/12pt Scala   *System* QuarkXPress®

A catalogue record for this book is available from the British Library

ISBN 0 521 53858 0 paperback

Cover image: © Getty Images/PhotoDisc

Contents

Introduction   **4**
    Before the play begins   5

Commentary   **6**

Contexts   **70**
    What did Shakespeare write?   70
    What did Shakespeare read?   71
    What was Shakespeare's England like?   74
      Queen Elizabeth I   75
      King James I   76
      King Christian IV   78
      Rome and Egypt   79
      Changing ideas of honour   80
    Shakespeare's own life   81

Language   **82**
    Imagery   82
    Antithesis   87
    Repetition   88
    Lists   90
    Verse and prose   91

Critical approaches   **92**
    Traditional criticism   92
    Modern criticism   96
      Political criticism   98
      Feminist criticism   100
      Performance criticism   103
      Psychoanalytic criticism   106
      Postmodern criticism   107

Organising your responses   **108**
    Writing about an extract   109
    Writing an essay   117
    Writing about character   122
    A note on examiners   124

Resources   **125**
    Books   125
    Films and audio books   128
    Antony and Cleopatra on the Web   128

Introduction

Antony and Cleopatra is full of contrasts which reinforce and comment upon each other. The most obvious opposition is that of Rome and Egypt. Rome values discipline, restraint, duty and bravery in war. Egypt values luxury, excess, play and emotional desire. Other contrasts set loyalty against betrayal, fertility against corruption, and, as the play harks back to what Antony once was, past versus present.

The play's ever-shifting, contradictory viewpoints similarly create very different perspectives on the two main characters and the nature of their love. Antony was traditionally seen as a great warrior who threw away the world for love. Besotted with Cleopatra, he lost his empire because of his passion. Once held to be like Mars and Hercules, his lust has transformed him into a 'strumpet's fool'. In like fashion, Cleopatra is both 'enchanting queen' and 'foul Egyptian'. The nature of Antony and Cleopatra's love is similarly contrasted. Some see it as lust, others as a magnificently heroic love affair.

Given such contradictory views, there are sharp divisions of opinion on what kind of play it is. *Antony and Cleopatra* has been variously categorised as a tragedy, a tragi-comedy, a history play, a morality play, a satire and a problem play. By providing such different perspectives, the openness of the play continually unsettles the judgements of audiences. Moral uncertainty is built into the fabric of the play: it is difficult to take what any speaker says at face value.

Each character possesses a distinctive language. Roman speech is spare; Egyptian speech is sensuous. Antony and Cleopatra indulge in soaring hyperbole as they express their emotions for each other or their attitudes to Rome and Egypt. The rich imagery likewise conveys the play's themes, particularly the recurring images of melting and dissolution which aptly express Antony's decline, his feeling of loss of identity, and his and Cleopatra's determination to die.

The play is both intimate and public: the love story and the struggle for political power are inextricably bound up together. The lovers are entangled in history: they make it and are unmade by it. That combination of political and personal instability and intrigue ensures that in performance *Antony and Cleopatra* proves a supremely moving and politically thought-provoking theatrical experience.

Before the play begins

Over 2000 years ago, Rome was the centre of an expanding military and economic empire. In 60 BC, Julius Caesar, Pompey and Crassus formed an alliance (the first Triumvirate, or 'rule by three') to share control of the Roman provinces. Crassus was killed during an expedition to subdue the Parthians (see Act 3 Scene 1, lines 1–5) and, soon after, Julius Caesar and Pompey clashed. Pompey was routed at the battle of Pharsalus in 48 BC. He fled to Egypt, where Cleopatra was embroiled in a power struggle with her brother, King Ptolemy. Ptolemy's supporters killed Pompey in the hope of gaining favour with Julius Caesar, who arrived in pursuit of Pompey.

Cleopatra quickly charmed Julius Caesar, who defeated Ptolemy and made her Queen of Egypt. They had a son, Caesarion. When Caesar returned to Rome, he was virtually sole master of the Roman Republic, a king in all but name. But the tensions and conflicts in Roman society were too strong to tolerate the rule of one man.

In 44 BC, a group of senators led by Brutus and Cassius assassinated Caesar on the day the Roman Senate was to proclaim him king. But the Republicans were not successful for long. Mark Antony took over the leadership of Caesar's supporters, aided by Octavius Caesar, the 19-year-old great-nephew and adopted son of Julius Caesar. Together they defeated Brutus and Cassius at the battle of Philippi. Shakespeare dramatises these events in *Julius Caesar*.

Mark Antony, Octavius Caesar and Lepidus (the second Triumvirate) shared out the Roman provinces between them. Antony agreed to pacify the eastern provinces, Lepidus controlled North Africa, while Octavius Caesar returned to Rome to suppress Sextus Pompeius (Pompey's son), who had taken Sicily, Corsica and Sardinia and was endangering the food supply of Rome. Antony's campaigns in the East led to his encounter with Cleopatra.

It is about 41 BC when *Antony and Cleopatra* opens. Mark Antony has abandoned his wife Fulvia and lives in Alexandria with Cleopatra. Elsewhere in the Roman world, the Triumvirate's hold on power is weakening. The Parthians continue to threaten its eastern provinces, Sextus Pompeius' fleet has mastery of the Mediterranean and there is civil unrest and rebellion within Italy. As Octavius Caesar and Lepidus struggle to keep control, Mark Antony, besotted with Cleopatra, remains in Egypt and does nothing.

Commentary

Act 1 Scene 1

> Nay, but this dotage of our general's
> O'erflows the measure. *(lines 1–2)*

The scene is set in Cleopatra's palace in Alexandria, and Philo's first words condemn Antony's infatuation with Cleopatra. Philo protests that Antony, once the model for all noble warriors, has lost all military qualities and has become merely 'the bellows and the fan / To cool a gipsy's lust'. It is significant that here Shakespeare provides a stage direction which is the visual equivalent of Philo's words, having Cleopatra enter *'with eunuchs fanning her'*. And the word 'gipsy' contemptuously reveals Rome's attitude to Egypt and her queen. Shakespeare uses the Roman Philo to open and close Scene 1 as a choric commentator. He exposes the vast gap in values and behaviour between Egypt and Rome. Philo invites Demetrius – and the audience – to witness Antony's degeneration from a triumvir (one of the three political masters of the world) into the plaything of a whore:

> Look where they come.
> Take but good note, and you shall see in him
> The triple pillar of the world transformed
> Into a strumpet's fool. Behold and see. *(lines 10–13)*

Every director considers carefully how to stage the audience's first sight of Antony and Cleopatra. Traditional productions often staged a ceremonial entrance of much grandeur and dignity, but most modern productions present the lovers playfully engaged with each other, locked in embrace or tugging at each other's clothing. In the 2002 Royal Shakespeare Company production, the lovers were already on stage, with Cleopatra sensuously rubbing oil into Antony's back. The dramatic intention was to give a context to their first exchange in which Cleopatra demands to know how much Antony loves her. Antony dismisses as worthless the value of love that can be calculated, and when Cleopatra claims she will set a limit ('bourn') on his love, he responds in a style that will characterise the whole play, hyperbole (obviously exaggerated language):

Then must thou needs find out new heaven, new earth.

(line 17)

The lovers' playful talk is interrupted by a messenger from Rome. Antony, irritated, demands to hear the news in brief, but Cleopatra mocks him, saying it is perhaps about his wife Fulvia's anger, or a peremptory command from young Caesar to conquer or liberate another kingdom. She continues to taunt him, claiming he blushes at the thought of being vassal ('homager') to Caesar or scolded by Fulvia. Cleopatra's teasing prompts Antony to another hyperbolic outburst:

Let Rome in Tiber melt and the wide arch
Of the ranged empire fall!

(lines 35–6)

In the same extravagant style, Antony declares he cares only to be with Cleopatra, embracing or kissing her as he claims, 'The nobleness of life / Is to do thus'. As if issuing a public proclamation, he calls on the world to recognise ('weet') that he and Cleopatra have no equals in love: 'We stand up peerless'. But Cleopatra continues to tease, accusing him of outrageous lying, 'Excellent falsehood!', and reminding him she is no fool like him. Antony protests he is 'stirred' (sexually excited) only by her, and proposes pleasure rather than 'conference harsh'. Looking forward to 'sport', he refuses to hear any message from Rome, praises Cleopatra, and declares that tonight they will wander the streets, observing the people of Alexandria. Shakespeare is using here a quotation from Plutarch (see page 71) which claimed that Antony and Cleopatra would sometimes disguise themselves as slaves to visit the city and watch and quarrel with its citizens.

Antony dismisses the messenger and the stage empties, leaving only Philo and Demetrius to comment with dismay on what they have seen and heard. Both note how slightly Antony values Caesar and that he no longer displays the greatness he once possessed. It confirms what malicious gossips have been saying in Rome. Demetrius' expression 'approves the common liar' (confirms what liars say is true) expresses another characteristic which will recur throughout the play: paradox. Neither Philo nor Demetrius will appear in the play again, but they have served their dramatic function to draw attention to:

- the vast difference between Egypt and Rome;
- Antony's change from noble soldier to infatuated lover;
- potential antagonism between Antony and Caesar.

Act 1 Scene 2

The first 70 lines of Scene 2 reveal the frivolous, pleasure-seeking, sexually obsessed nature of Cleopatra's court. Charmian and Iras, ladies-in-waiting to the queen, joke together as their fortunes are told by the Soothsayer. His formally spoken prophecies contain ominous meanings, but the two women refuse to see any menace in his words. Both women's chatter is full of sexual innuendo: 'figs' were thought to look like vaginas; 'an oily palm' was believed to signify sensuality; Iras' claim that she would prefer an inch 'Not in my husband's nose' is obviously a phallic joke; and both women tease Alexas unmercifully about his future as a cuckold (deceived husband). Their banter is interrupted by Cleopatra, who is evidently concerned about a change in Antony:

> He was disposed to mirth, but on the sudden
> A Roman thought hath struck him. *(lines 77–8)*

Antony is seen approaching, but Cleopatra determines not to speak with him, and the entire court exits with her, leaving only Antony and the messenger on stage. It is an abrupt mood change, as the relaxed atmosphere of Egypt gives way to Antony's 'Roman thought': reminders of duty, discipline and military affairs. The world of politics is forcing itself into the scene, opposing the preoccupation with love and idle pleasure the play has so far presented. Antony hears the news that the armies of his wife and brother have fought against each other, but then united to fight Octavius Caesar, who has defeated them and driven them out of Italy. The messenger has even worse news, but is afraid to tell it because it might cause him to be punished. Antony's order that he should report it reveals the stoical and fearless nature of his character (and is in marked contrast with how Cleopatra will treat a messenger who brings bad news in Act 2 Scene 5):

Things that are past are done, with me. 'Tis thus:
Who tells me true, though in his tale lie death,
I hear him as he flattered.   *(lines 93–5)*

The messenger reports that the victorious Parthians have occupied
Roman provinces from Syria to the shores of Asia (modern Turkey).
Antony knows that what the messenger is still afraid to report is that
such Roman defeats are due to his (Antony's) neglect of his military
obligations. He also knows that everyone in Rome is blaming his
infatuation with Cleopatra for his dereliction of duty, and he demands
that the messenger scold him just as Fulvia would. But he dismisses
the messenger and, as he waits for further news, determines to
abandon his life of lust and ease with Cleopatra and return to his
political and military responsibilities as a Roman:

These strong Egyptian fetters I must break,
Or lose myself in dotage.   *(lines 112–13)*

As he makes his resolve, yet another messenger brings news of
Fulvia's death. Antony is moved to regret. Although he had often
wished his wife dead, he now wishes her alive again. The thought
prompts him again to reflect on his own state, and he feels the
'present pleasure' of Egypt losing its attraction. He resolves again to
leave Cleopatra, 'I must from this enchanting queen break off', and
tells Enobarbus his decision. Enobarbus makes a joke of it, saying
Cleopatra will react passionately to his departure. He puns on 'dies'
and 'dying', which Shakespeare's audiences knew could mean 'reach
sexual orgasm'. Antony, seemingly preoccupied, merely responds,
'She is cunning past man's thought.' His words prompt Enobarbus to
describe Cleopatra in what will be seen to be his typically sardonic
style, as he ridicules Cleopatra's extreme feelings:

Alack, sir, no, her passions are made of nothing but the finest
part of pure love. We cannot call her winds and waters sighs
and tears; they are greater storms and tempests than almanacs
can report.   *(lines 142–5)*

Enobarbus similarly mocks Antony's fervent wish, 'Would I had never
seen her!' On hearing of Fulvia's death, Enobarbus offers consolation

in the same flippant manner. He says that the gods are the world's tailors, constantly fashioning new people to replace the old and worn-out, and so it is easy to find a new woman: Antony has a 'new petticoat' (Cleopatra) to replace his 'old smock' (Fulvia). Enobarbus ends with the cynical comment, 'the tears live in an onion that should water this sorrow'. But Antony's mind is now on political business. He proposes to inform Cleopatra why he must leave: not only because of Fulvia, but because Sextus Pompeius (Pompey, younger son of Pompey the Great) is gathering support from Rome's 'slippery people' to challenge Caesar. All-powerful at sea, Pompey lays claim to being the greatest soldier, and threatens the whole Roman empire. Antony's image of Pompey as 'like the courser's hair' is based on the contemporary belief that the hair of a horse ('courser'), when placed in water, grows into a serpent. Pompey, son of a mighty father, represents just such a growing threat to Rome. Antony orders Enobarbus to prepare his followers to leave with him for Rome.

Act 1 Scene 3

Throughout Scene 3, Cleopatra will deliberately goad Antony, pretend indifference, feign illness and variously be scornful, reproachful and sarcastic. Her order to Alexas to find Antony vividly reveals that she proposes to vex his emotions:

> See where he is, who's with him, what he does.
> I did not send you. If you find him sad,
> Say I am dancing; if in mirth, report
> That I am sudden sick. (lines 2–5)

Charmian attempts, without success, to advise Cleopatra that the best way to keep Antony's love is by not provoking him and by always giving in to him. Cleopatra dismisses the advice as foolish, and as Antony enters she begins to use all her wiles to prevent him from leaving. Her capriciousness is evident throughout the scene. She protests she is 'sick and sullen', pretends faintness and asks Charmian to help her away, then bids Antony to stand further away from her. She taunts him, accusing him of hearing good news from Fulvia, whom she contemptuously describes as 'the married woman'.

Cleopatra gives Antony no opportunity to talk about his departure as she declares she is 'mightily betrayed'. Antony has sworn false love to Fulvia and to herself in 'mouth-made vows' which involve only his lips, not his heart. As Antony tries to speak, she dismisses him and derisively reminds him of the hyperbolic language he had used when he first wooed her, describing the timeless beauty of her face, the joy of her eyebrow's arch, and her divine origin:

> Eternity was in our lips and eyes,
> Bliss in our brows' bent; none our parts so poor
> But was a race of heaven. *(lines 35–7)*

Cleopatra claims that her beauty remains so still, or else Antony is the world's greatest liar. She threatens that were she a man she would prove her bravery: 'I would I had thy inches.' At last Antony manages to explain, and tries to assure her of his love. The desperate situation in Rome calls him home, but his heart remains with her. He tells of factional war: 'Our Italy / Shines o'er with civil swords'. Sextus Pompeius, increasingly supported by dissident Romans, threatens Rome itself. Antony declares that peace itself grows sick and must be purged by the blood-letting of war, an image drawn from common medical practice in Shakespeare's time. Finally, he tells Cleopatra of Fulvia's death, but that news only provokes her to another outburst against Antony.

Cleopatra seems at first to disbelieve that Fulvia is dead, but then criticises Antony for not weeping for his wife, and declares that he will display the same lack of grief at her own death. Antony again protests his commitment to Cleopatra, swearing by 'the fire / That quickens Nilus' slime' (the sun that creates life in the mud of the Nile valley) that he will follow her desires in peace and war. But Cleopatra continues her provocation, chiding and cajoling in turn. She is clearly still putting into practice the strategy with which she began the scene, intent on irritating and tormenting Antony, refusing to accept his protestations of love or loyalty. She sarcastically reproaches him that she has learned the value of his love from Fulvia, bids him weep for Fulvia, and mocks his honour as deceitful play-acting:

> Good now, play one scene
> Of excellent dissembling, and let it look
> Like perfect honour. *(lines 78–80)*

The insult to his honour angers Antony, but Cleopatra is unmoved, scornfully calling him 'this herculean Roman', who is merely pretending rage (her description ridicules Antony's claim to be descended from the Greek hero Hercules). Cleopatra at last accepts that Antony is determined to leave, and she uses simple, direct language as she searches for the right words to say farewell. But she cannot resist adding a barbed comment that her memory, like Antony himself, has deserted her:

> Sir, you and I must part, but that's not it;
> Sir, you and I have loved, but there's not it;
> That you know well. Something it is I would –
> O, my oblivion is a very Antony,
> And I am all forgotten.   *(lines 88–92)*

In performance, Cleopatra's speech can be a poignant moment as she drops her play-acting and struggles to speak sincerely. However, some Cleopatras speak lines 91–92 reproachfully, as a further twist of the knife into Antony's emotions. Antony's response suggests that he feels scornfully rebuked by her words: he accuses her of 'idleness' (pretence), but Cleopatra gives the word a different meaning as she claims such 'idleness' (love) is as painful to her as giving birth. She asks forgiveness and wishes him success; but Shakespeare then gives her words that can be spoken, if an actress chooses, in a way that continues to mock Antony's honour, feigns self-pity, and heaps heavy irony upon her wish for his victory:

> Your honour calls you hence;
> Therefore be deaf to my unpitied folly,
> And all the gods go with you! Upon your sword
> Sit laurel victory, and smooth success
> Be strewed before your feet!   *(lines 98–102)*

Antony leaves, still swearing that even in their separation, he and Cleopatra will always be together in each other's hearts.

Act 1 Scene 4

Shakespeare now provides the audience with its first sight of Rome. Just as Philo opened the play condemning Antony's decline, now

Caesar even more strongly laments Antony's abandonment of Roman values for the debauched pleasures of Egypt. Caesar and Lepidus are Antony's fellow triumvirs (three rulers of the Roman world), and Scene 4 will reveal that, whereas Lepidus views Antony's behaviour leniently, Caesar is unequivocal in his puritanical disapproval. He condemns Antony's merry-making and neglect of his political duties as conduct ill-befitting a Roman male:

> he fishes, drinks, and wastes
> The lamps of night in revel; is not more manlike
> Than Cleopatra, nor the queen of Ptolemy
> More womanly than he; hardly gave audience, or
> Vouchsafed to think he had partners.   *(lines 4–8)*

Lepidus attempts to defend Antony, saying it is because of his goodness that his faults appear so starkly, just as stars appear bright against the black night sky. But Caesar rebukes Lepidus for being too indulgent of Antony's character. In performance, the disdain in his voice is obvious as he says it might be possible to excuse Antony's sexual adventures with Cleopatra, his rewarding of a joke with a kingdom, his drinking with slaves and sweaty commoners. Caesar is speaking with bitter irony, and clearly thinks such behaviour repulsive and non-excusable. But he directly condemns Antony's abandonment of his obligations as triumvir, leaving Caesar to cope with the present political and military troubles: 'we do bear / So great weight in his lightness'.

Clearly exasperated, Caesar wishes that Antony would confine his pleasure-seeking to his leisure time ('vacancy'), when he would deserve no more than the belly-aches and syphilis ('dryness of his bones') that might result. But to waste time when the fate of the Triumvirate is at stake is to deserve to be rebuked like a boy who, old enough to know better, seeks immediate gratification of his desires. Again it is evident that it is Antony's neglect of the Roman values of duty, self-restraint and discipline that vexes Caesar. The need for such qualities at this time is made even more pressing by the messenger's news: Sextus Pompeius (Pompey) has a powerful fleet and disaffected Romans are flocking to his cause. The news prompts Caesar to reflect on the fickleness of the common people of Rome, comparing them to a reed ('flag') in a river, moving back and forth with the tide, like a lackey (servile servant) following any master:

> This common body,
> Like to a vagabond flag upon the stream,
> Goes to and back, lackeying the varying tide
> To rot itself with motion.   *(lines 44–7)*

More bad news arrives. Pompey's allies, the pirates Menecrates and Menas, threaten the coasts of Italy. They attract fresh recruits, and capture ships at will. Pompey's cause flourishes. The news makes Caesar wish even more fervently for Antony to abandon Cleopatra and return to defend Rome: 'Antony, / Leave thy lascivious wassails.' Caesar recalls how great a general Antony once was, courageous and unafraid of any hardship. He describes how Antony slew two consuls in battle, and in the retreat across the Alps that followed, uncomplainingly endured thirst and famine. He drank horse's urine and scum-covered water, and ate berries and the bark of trees.

Caesar fervently hopes that Antony's 'shames' will drive him swiftly to Rome to face the threat of Pompey. Caesar's Roman qualities of military valour, discipline, efficiency and distrust of 'idleness' are evident in his abrupt words to Lepidus:

> 'Tis time we twain
> Did show ourselves i'th'field, and to that end
> Assemble we immediate council. Pompey
> Thrives in our idleness.   *(lines 75–8)*

Act 1 Scene 5

The contrast with the preceding scene is marked. Caesar's Rome is characterised by urgency and action, but Scene 5 shows Cleopatra seeking to while away the time until Antony returns. Here, Egypt displays the idleness that Caesar so much abhors. Cleopatra drowsily longs for mandragora (a narcotic plant) so that she can sleep out the time until Antony returns. She jokes with Mardian the eunuch about his sexual impotence ('unseminared' means 'castrated'). Mardian claims to have 'fierce affections' and reminds Cleopatra of 'What Venus did with Mars'. His reference is to the well-known story in classical mythology of how the goddess of love seduced the god of war. Here, as throughout the play, Shakespeare seems to be encouraging the audience to associate Antony and Cleopatra with Mars and Venus: a mighty warrior made ridiculous by love.

Cleopatra wonders what Antony is doing, and the thought of him riding is turned into a sexual image: 'O happy horse, to bear the weight of Antony!' She daydreams about Antony's heroic qualities: in her eyes, he is like Atlas, an armed protector and supporter of the world. She fantasises that Antony is thinking of her ('Where's my serpent of old Nile?') and gives an unflattering description of herself as she invites him to think of her as deeply sunburnt and aged: 'with Phoebus' amorous pinches black / And wrinkled deep in time'.

Still deep in her lethargic daydream, Cleopatra recalls her affair with Julius Caesar and how she enchanted Pompey. Her reverie is interrupted by Alexas, who brings a pearl from Antony, and repeats Antony's promise to add kingdoms to Cleopatra's empire, making her mistress of all the East. Alexas' description of Antony as 'nor sad nor merry' evokes an enthusiastic response from his mistress that praises Antony and reassures her of his love: 'O well-divided disposition!'

Cleopatra, who has already sent many letters to Antony, resolves to write to him yet again. Charmian teases her about her love for Julius Caesar, but Cleopatra threatens her with 'bloody teeth' if she dares compare Antony with Caesar. The rebuke may be seriously or playfully spoken in performance. Charmian's half-mocking apology ('I sing but after you') prompts Cleopatra to dismiss her affair with Caesar as mere youthful inexperience. Her dismissal is expressed in one of the play's most memorable images, implying just how 'green' she was at the time:

> My salad days,
> When I was green in judgement   *(lines 76–7)*

Cleopatra ends the scene determined to send Antony several letters each day, which she expresses with typical hyperbole: if she doesn't fulfil her vow, she will kill all her subjects:

> He shall have every day a several greeting,
> Or I'll unpeople Egypt.   *(lines 80–1)*

Act 1: Critical review

Act 1 displays crucial features that will run through the whole play: the opposition of Rome and Egypt, Antony's decline from great general to infatuated lover, and rivalry between Antony and Caesar. In the opening scene, the disapproving Philo pithily expresses the Roman perspective on Antony, which Caesar echoes in Scene 4. The once mighty Antony has fallen under the seductive spell of Cleopatra and now neglects his duties as triumvir in favour of the dissipation of 'lascivious wassails': sexual indulgence and drunken revelling.

The stark contrast of Rome and Egypt is evident. Rome represents the 'serious' world of politics, male honour and emotional control. In contrast, Scene 2 establishes Egypt as a world of play: sensuous, feminine, passionate. Antony clearly perceives his divided allegiance, caught between duty and desire: 'I must from this enchanting queen break off.' But Act 1 demonstrates that his resolve to forsake Cleopatra is a delusion: his love and lust for her must prevail.

That unbreakable emotional entanglement is, however, set firmly in the world of politics. Events press in on the lovers: the wars of Antony's brother and Fulvia against Caesar, the invasion by the Parthians, Fulvia's death, the growing threat of Pompey, and the unreliable loyalties of the Roman citizens. As the play progresses, the love affair will become ever more caught up in a struggle for political mastery of the whole world.

Shakespeare establishes the vastness of that world in his use of messengers. In four of the five scenes, messengers bring news. It is a theatrical device that will recur throughout the play to create a sense of scale and urgency and to advance the action. Just as importantly, Shakespeare uses hyperbole to portray the cosmic scale of Antony and Cleopatra's love. Their aggrandised visions of each other may be self-deluding, but their conception of the superhuman nature of their love is evident in their first exchange (Scene 1, lines 14–17):

CLEOPATRA If it be love indeed, tell me how much.
ANTONY There's beggary in the love that can be reckoned.
CLEOPATRA I'll set a bourn how far to be beloved.
ANTONY Then must thou needs find out new heaven, new earth.

Act 2 Scene 1

Scene 1 provides the first sight of the men who challenge the supremacy of Rome's Triumvirate: Pompey and his allies, the pirates Menecrates and Menas. The 1993 Royal Shakespeare Company production set the scene on Pompey's galley, caught in a storm at sea. Pompey is confident that his rebellion is just and is sure that 'the great gods' will assist him, but is impatient for their help. He lists the factors that favour him: the people's love, his control of the sea, his growing ('crescent') army, Antony's absence in Egypt, Caesar's unpopularity, and Lepidus' poor reputation with his fellow triumvirs. Pompey hopes that Cleopatra's lascivious ('Salt') enchantment will keep Antony in Egypt. His words portray both Cleopatra's erotic appeal and Antony's physical and sexual appetite that suspends his sense of honour:

> Let witchcraft joined with beauty, lust with both,
> Tie up the libertine in a field of feasts,
> Keep his brain fuming. Epicurean cooks,
> Sharpen with cloyless sauce his appetite,
> That sleep and feeding may prorogue his honour
> Even till a Lethe'd dullness – *(lines 22–7)*

Epicurus was a philosopher who recommended a life of sensual pleasure, and Lethe was a river in Hades (hell) from which the dead drank and forgot their past life. Pompey's hope that Antony still revels in Egypt is immediately shattered by what Varrius reports: Antony will soon be in Rome. The news dismays Pompey, and he praises Antony as a far superior soldier than Caesar or Lepidus. But Pompey gains some comfort from the fact that Antony's presence acknowledges the power of his (Pompey's) challenge. Menas adds further comfort by suggesting that Caesar and Antony will surely quarrel, but Pompey suspects that the Triumvirate may now unite against him. He ends the scene with a couplet, putting his fortune in the hands of the gods, but also expressing a steely resolve to fight to the utmost of his power:

> Be't as our gods will have't! It only stands
> Our lives upon to use our strongest hands. *(lines 51–2)*

Act 2 Scene 2

The scene opens with Lepidus clearly hoping to heal the rift between Antony and Caesar. He urges Enobarbus to advise Antony to restrain his anger when he meets Caesar. Enobarbus' response is blunt and unhelpful. He will entreat Antony 'To answer like himself': to reply in warlike terms ('speak as loud as Mars') if Caesar angers him. Lepidus tries again, saying this is not the time for personal resentments or small matters, but again Enobarbus rejects a conciliatory approach, leaving Lepidus to beg him not to inflame Antony's rage: 'stir / No embers up'.

Shakespeare now has Antony and Caesar enter, but ensures that in performance they studiously ignore each other. Each man is in conversation with a subordinate, and neither triumvir acknowledges the presence of the other. It is left to Lepidus to bring the two together, and he does so in his familiar peace-making manner, urging them to remember their former great alliance and not be divided by unimportant matters. Just how each man responds is up to the actors. Shakespeare gives them seemingly conciliatory words, but the lines can be spoken and acted to convey any attitude from genuine friendship to scarcely veiled hostility. (For example, just what does Antony do as he says 'thus'?)

ANTONY   'Tis spoken well.
    Were we before our armies, and to fight,
    I should do thus.
CAESAR Welcome to Rome.   *(lines 27–30)*

What happens next shows that neither man is reconciled to the other. There is a brief episode (often comic in performance) in which each invites the other to 'Sit', struggling partly to show courtesy, but mainly to establish just who is the superior, entitled to give the other an order. Then Antony takes the initiative, determined to bring grievances into the open and to remind Caesar that what he does in Egypt is none of Caesar's business.

Caesar cleverly avoids the challenge. He says small things do not concern him; he would be laughed at if he took them seriously. He would not criticise Antony over matters that are no concern of his. But Antony is not placated by Caesar's half-flattering response, and bluntly asks how his being in Egypt might concern Caesar. Again

Caesar answers diplomatically ('No more than my residing here at Rome / Might be to you in Egypt'), but then forces the issue:

> Yet if you there
> Did practise on my state, your being in Egypt
> Might be my question. *(lines 44–6)*

The word 'practise' (plot against) inflames Antony and he demands to know Caesar's meaning. Caesar makes it clear, claiming that Antony's brother and wife made war against him, incited by Antony himself. Antony denies the allegation: he had no part in his brother's rebellion, which injured him as much as it did Caesar, and his earlier letters to Caesar showed that. But Antony's reply does not placate Caesar, who now accuses Antony of calling his (Caesar's) judgement into question. Antony protests again, claiming Caesar must have understood that wars against Caesar were equally wars against him as fellow triumvir ('partner'). Antony then turns to the matter of Fulvia's rebellion and, using the image of a horse restrained by a bridle bit ('snaffle'), claims she was impossible to control. In effect he says to Caesar, I wish you had a wife like her, then you could understand my difficulties. His words prompt a typically sardonic comment from Enobarbus:

> Would we had all such wives, that the men might go to wars
> with the women! *(lines 71–2)*

Antony, still on the defensive, continues to blame Fulvia's uncontrollability, and acknowledges the distress her 'garboils' (rebellions) caused Caesar. He protests it was not his fault. But Caesar coldly reminds him of the time when, 'rioting in Alexandria' (debauching himself in Egypt), Antony insultingly refused to receive Caesar's messages from his messenger. Antony seems to try to bluster his way out of the accusation, blaming the messenger's lack of courtesy, and claiming he had a hangover from the previous night's entertainment of three kings. There is a hollowness in Antony's explanation, and the audience has seen how Antony actually treated the messenger in Act 1 Scene 1. Antony's makeshift excuses suggest a petty, non-heroic aspect of his character.

Caesar now makes his most serious charge: Antony has not

behaved like a Roman; he has broken his oath, a thing Caesar would never do. Lepidus recognises the danger in levelling such an accusation and urges caution: 'Soft, Caesar!' But Antony, his honour questioned, demands to know just why Caesar feels he has not kept his word. Caesar's reason is brief and direct: Antony refused to send 'arms and aid' when Caesar asked. Again Antony tries to wriggle out of the charge. But he then seems almost to accept responsibility, repenting his conduct ('play the penitent') and, whilst insisting on his honesty, offers a near apology to Caesar and asks pardon for his being the unwitting cause ('ignorant motive') of Fulvia's rebellion.

Antony's admission, and his plea for pardon, may be cynical political manouevres, but many critics interpret them as sincerely offered. The episode has often been interpreted as revealing Antony's nobility, in contrast to Caesar's inflexible pursuit of his complaints and lack of response to Antony's request for pardon (but it should be noted that some critics argue that Antony's intention throughout is always to shift blame from himself). Both Lepidus and Maecenas accept Antony's words at their face value, and see them as a way out, leaving the triumvirs free to deal with the current crisis of Pompey's rebellion. But Enobarbus is, as usual, much more cynical, and suggests that Antony and Caesar should just pretend friendship until Pompey is defeated. After that they 'shall have time to wrangle'.

Enobarbus' cynicism proves to be well-founded as Caesar makes clear he thinks reconciliation is impossible because of his and Antony's very different temperaments. But in one of the 'world' images that characterise the whole play (here the image is of a metal hoop that keeps a barrel watertight), Caesar claims he would, if he could, seek to restore their unity:

> Yet if I knew
> What hoop should hold us staunch, from edge to edge
> O'th'world I would pursue it.   *(lines 121–3)*

Caesar's claim prompts Agrippa to suggest a strategy that will bind the two world leaders together: Antony should marry Octavia, Caesar's sister. Caesar's response is to jibe about Cleopatra, but Antony, perhaps seeing political advantage, asks Agrippa to explain further. Agrippa's proposal is full of expressions that signify the unity the marriage will effect between Antony and Caesar: 'perpetual amity', 'make you brothers', 'knit your hearts', 'all loves to both'. He praises Octavia's beauty, flatters Antony and assures both men that the marriage will remove 'All little jealousies' and 'all great fears' between them.

Antony and Caesar are both cautious and wary, unwilling to respond until the other man has spoken. But when Caesar shows he is ready to accept Agrippa's plan, Antony whole-heartedly agrees, calling the politically arranged marriage an 'act of grace', and praying that

> from this hour
> The heart of brothers govern in our loves
> And sway our great designs!   *(lines 156–8)*

The two 'world-sharers' shake hands on the bargain, with Caesar expressing brotherly love for his sister and a wish that the marriage will permanently seal up his alliance and friendship with Antony. The moment has great dramatic potential because in performance the actors can subtly suggest that both men remain suspicious of each other in spite of their carefully chosen words that signify amity. In a 1987 production, Caesar flinched from contact as he offered his hand.

Their thoughts now turn to Pompey. Antony comments on the kindnesses Pompey has shown towards him, but joins with Caesar in planning to attack Pompey after the marriage (which Antony revealingly calls 'The business').

Their political and personal differences now seemingly resolved, the triumvirs depart, leaving only Enobarbus, Agrippa and Maecenas on stage: a hard-headed professional soldier and two skilful politicians. Their conversation is in stark and ironic contrast to what the audience has just seen and heard, exposing Caesar's and Antony's political alliance through Octavia as already fated to fail. They relax in gossip about Egypt, and the two politicians express wonder at reports of a fabulous banquet there. Enobarbus lightly dismisses the description of the feast as understatement, and the talk turns to Cleopatra, 'a most triumphant lady', a description that bodes ominously for Octavia. As Enobarbus tells of Antony's first meeting with Cleopatra upon the river of Cydnus, Shakespeare makes clear that the political marriage of convenience that has just been arranged between Antony and Octavia will not last. Antony cannot break free from Cleopatra's seductive magnetism.

Shakespeare based Enobarbus' lines on his reading of Plutarch, and you can find on pages 72–3 how he transformed Plutarch's prose into inspired verse. It is impossible to summarise Enobarbus' speech (lines 201–28) without trivialising the quality of its poetic expression, but the following images and phrases in particular capture the opulence and sensuality of Cleopatra's theatrical presentation of herself, staged to entrap Antony:

- 'like a burnished throne' (line 201) – a setting fit for a goddess;
- 'Burned on the water' (line 202) – hinting at the heat of passion;
- 'so perfumèd that / The winds were lovesick with them' (lines 203–4) – an overpowering, drug-like effect, enchantingly seductive;
- 'As amorous of their strokes' (line 207) – even the water cannot resist the sexual lure associated with Cleopatra, expressed in movement and music;
- 'It beggared all description' (line 208) – there are simply no words that can do justice to Cleopatra;
- 'cloth of gold, of tissue' (line 209) – suggesting both fabulous wealth and very ostentatious self-presentation;
- 'O'erpicturing that Venus where we see / The fancy outwork nature' (lines 210–11) – Cleopatra presents herself as though she were a work of art, outdoing any portrait of the goddess of love, Venus;
- 'like smiling Cupids' (line 212) – another carefully arranged reminder of love;
- 'And what they undid did' (line 215) – suggesting Cleopatra's paradoxical appeal, able to simultaneously create and convey opposites (as the fans both 'glow' and 'cool' her cheeks) – the antithesis 'undid did' is typical of the play's style (see pages 87–8);
- 'like the Nereides, / So many mermaids' (lines 216–17) – the Nereides are sea-nymphs – throughout the play, Cleopatra is associated with water – impossible to grasp, flowing, changing, universally experienced but always somehow mysterious;
- 'And made their bends adornings' (line 218) – suggesting all creatures bow in graceful postures to the queen;
- 'Swell with the touches of those flower-soft hands' (line 220) – an erotically suggestive image of how the very rigging of the barge is stirred to sensual feeling by the 'seeming mermaid' who steers;

- 'A strange invisible perfume' (line 222) – the narcotic atmosphere that surrounds Cleopatra, excuding a mysterious and overpowering odour;
- 'The city cast / Her people out upon her' (lines 223–4) – Cleopatra attracts acclaim from everyone, and no one can resist her;
- 'did sit alone' (line 225) – Antony, one of the three most powerful men in the world, cannot attract a single person to see him when there is the chance of seeing the fabulous queen of Egypt;
- 'And made a gap in nature' (line 228) – even the air itself 'Had gone to gaze on Cleopatra'.

Cleopatra's appearance at Cydnus had been magnificently stage-managed, and her dazzling presentation utterly upstaged Antony, leaving him alone, whistling to the air. Enobarbus goes on to describe how she gained further advantage over Antony, declining his invitation to supper and suggesting he come to dine with her. Enobarbus returns to his usual sardonic style as he describes Antony as a man 'Whom ne'er the word of "No" woman heard speak', and how he 'barbered ten times o'er', went to Cleopatra's feast, and 'for his ordinary' (the price of his meal), paid his heart.

Agrippa uses an earthy image of ploughing and cropping to tell how Cleopatra had earlier snared Julius Caesar and had children by him. His words prompt Enobarbus to recall how he once saw Cleopatra 'Hop forty paces through the public street', but even in that outrageous behaviour she made 'defect perfection'. Once again the antithesis catches Cleopatra's contradictory nature: even when she was breathless she could 'power breathe forth'. Maecenas, reflecting on the coming marriage of Antony and Octavia, declares that Antony must now leave his Egyptian queen. Enobarbus' response is blunt and confident: 'Never. He will not.' He goes on to provide the play's most memorable summary of Cleopatra's vitality and appeal:

> Age cannot wither her, nor custom stale
> Her infinite variety. Other women cloy
> The appetites they feed, but she makes hungry
> Where most she satisfies. *(lines 245–8)*

Shakespeare is making it plain to the audience that Antony, in thrall to such attractions, will return to Cleopatra. Even though Maecenas speaks of Octavia's 'beauty, wisdom, modesty', it is clear that she stands no chance of keeping Antony in Rome. He will be drawn back to Egypt by Cleopatra's 'infinite variety'.

Act 2 Scene 3

Scene 3 provides an immediate ironic confirmation of what the audience has just heard, by opening with Antony telling Octavia his affairs as triumvir will sometimes take him away from her. The irony deepens as he urges her not to believe rumours about his past improper behaviour (the expression 'have not kept my square' refers to the use of a set-square to draw perfect architectural diagrams) and then promises that everything he does in the future will be done 'by th'rule' (the sense of 'keeping on the straight and narrow' echoes the set-square image of drawing straight lines). Shakespeare adds even more irony to the scene by beginning with the stage direction that Octavia should enter 'between' Antony and Caesar: a dramatic representation of the fact that she is a woman trapped between two powerful men, her husband and her brother. Both are using her as a political counter, and her loyalty to both will be strained to the utmost.

Caesar and Octavia leave, and Antony questions the Soothsayer, who advises him to return to Egypt because if he stays in Rome he will be overshadowed by Caesar. Although Antony's guardian spirit ('daemon') has great qualities, 'Noble, courageous, high unmatchable', whenever Caesar is near it loses all its powers. Antony's brightness dims in the shadow of Caesar: 'Thy lustre thickens / When he shines by.' Antony recognises the truth of the warning. His sense of feeling inferior to Caesar is obvious as he reflects upon how he loses at gambling and cock-fighting. Shakespeare emphatically reinforces the ironic tone of the scene as Antony declares a decision which denies all he has just said to Octavia, exposes the *realpolitik* of the arranged marriage and confirms all Enobarbus said of Cleopatra in the previous scene:

> I will to Egypt;
> And though I make this marriage for my peace,
> I'th'East my pleasure lies.   *(lines 38–40)*

Even in what seems such a personal moment, Shakespeare keeps the world-encompassing political range of the play in focus. The scene ends with Antony dispatching Ventidius to crush the revolt of the Parthians against the Roman empire.

Act 2 Scene 4

Like the final three lines of Scene 3, this brief scene reminds the audience of Rome's power, efficiency and determination to quell any political and military challenge. Lepidus urges Agrippa and Maecenas to join Antony and Caesar at Misena to fight with Pompey.

Act 2 Scene 5

After the brisk, business-like Roman politics of the preceding four scenes, Scene 5 returns to Egypt. Broody and sultry, Cleopatra, waiting for Antony, seeks diversion to pass away the time. She calls for music, describing it in one of the play's many images of eating as 'moody food / Of us that trade in love'. She jokes about Mardian's impotence – a eunuch has nothing that can satisfy her. She thinks of going fishing, where each fish she catches will remind her of her absent lover:

> I'll think them every one an Antony
> And say, 'Aha! You're caught.'   *(lines 14–15)*

Charmian tries to distract her mistress, reminding her of the trick she played on Antony, using a diver to hang a fish on the end of his line. Cleopatra enjoys the memory: 'That time? – O times!' and recalls other past pleasures, the amorous games they played. She had out-drunk him, dressed him in her clothes, and worn his sword, with which he had won the battle of Philippi (dramatised by Shakespeare in *Julius Caesar*). Jacobeans would have recognised in this anecdote yet another association of Antony with Hercules (see page 49). According to Roman legend, Hercules was bewitched by Omphale, who dressed him in her clothes while she wore his lion skin and helmet and wielded his club.

Reality now intrudes into Cleopatra's daydreaming as a messenger arrives. She fears at once that something is wrong. Is Antony dead? Cleopatra's emotions swing wildly as she first says that such news would kill her, then says that she will give gold and offer her hand (that trembling kings have kissed) for the messenger to kiss if he reports that Antony lives. Cleopatra's volatile emotions are shown in her response to the messenger's reassurance that Antony is well. She threatens dreadful punishment (that was actually meted out to the wealthy Roman Crassus):

> Why, there's more gold. But, sirrah, mark, we use
> To say the dead are well. Bring it to that,
> The gold I give thee will I melt and pour
> Down thy ill-uttering throat. *(lines 32–5)*

The messenger tries to give his news, but Cleopatra is caught up in her fantasies and fears. She declares the messenger's face looks too sour ('tart') to report good news, then says that if the news is bad he should come 'like a Fury': a spirit of vengeance from the underworld, dressed all in black and with writhing serpents in place of hair. Again the messenger pleads to give his report, and again Cleopatra unleashes a torrent of threats and promises of reward, one moment seeming about to strike him, the next promising to set him in 'a shower of gold' and give him rich pearls. The messenger delivers his news in small items: Antony is well, friends with Caesar, even friendlier than before. Cleopatra rewards each tiny item with praise, but the messenger knows he has got to the point where he must deliver the news that will provoke Cleopatra's ungovernable wrath again. Two short lines create a delicious moment of theatre:

MESSENGER   But yet, madam –
CLEOPATRA I do not like 'But yet'   *(lines 50–1)*

In performance there is often a highly charged pause after Cleopatra's ominous declaration of her dislike. The audience savours the anticipation of the fury that is about to descend on the hapless (and totally innocent) messenger. Cleopatra embroiders on her distaste for 'But yet', gives a quick recap of what she has gathered so far, then demands that the messenger should make all clear. Shakespeare strings out the suspense a little longer, leading up to the messenger's admission that Antony is bound to Octavia 'For the best turn i'th'bed.' It is a curious way of reporting the marriage. Some messengers have delivered the line in an apologetic, half-joking way, before stating plainly that Antony is married to Octavia. The effect on Cleopatra is cataclysmic:

The most infectious pestilence upon thee!   *(line 62)*

Cleopatra strikes the messenger, abuses him, threatens to tear out his eyes and 'unhair' his head. She seizes him and drags him around by the hair, still shrieking dire threats:

> Thou shalt be whipped with wire, and stewed in brine,
> Smarting in ling'ring pickle!   *(lines 66–7)*

The messenger's all too reasonable reply stands in marked contrast to Cleopatra's inflamed language. It expresses the condition of all such messengers who report bad news, and it usually provokes much laughter among modern audiences:

> Gracious madam,
> I that do bring the news made not the match.   *(lines 67–8)*

But Cleopatra is still completely possessed by her ever-changing passions. She promises to make the messenger ruler of a province if he will only say it is not so. When the messenger confirms yet again that Antony is married, she draws a knife and threatens to kill him. He runs off and Charmian tries to reason with her mistress, reminding her that the messenger is innocent. Charmian's attempt to calm Cleopatra results only in another hyperbolic outburst:

> Some innocents scape not the thunderbolt.
> Melt Egypt into Nile, and kindly creatures
> Turn all to serpents!   *(lines 78–80)*

Her mood changes and, calmer, she sends for the messenger and expresses regret at having struck an inferior. He returns, often in performance evoking audience laughter by clearly showing his fear that he is about to be punished yet again. Cleopatra struggles to control her temper as she questions him, still evidently hoping against hope that he has been lying. But the messenger confirms the truth of his report, and narrowly escapes another beating as Cleopatra explodes, 'The gods confound thee'. She finally accepts the reality that she has lost Antony, and lets fly another searing curse upon her country:

> So half my Egypt were submerged and made
> A cistern for scaled snakes!   *(lines 96–7)*

Once again Cleopatra comments on how ugly the messenger appears to her, and twice demands to have him confirm that Antony is married. She at last dismisses him with a wish that he be ruined by the news he has brought. Her passionate hysteria subsides, but she continues to display the self-obsessed, capricious aspect of her nature, praising her old love, Julius Caesar, above Antony. She then sends Alexas to question the messenger about Octavia's looks, age and temperament. Wishing to know all about the rival who she thinks has stolen Antony from her, she adds a final detail: 'Let him not leave out / The colour of her hair.'

Her violent mood swings return as she wishes Antony gone for ever, then immediately revokes that wish: 'Let him not'. In a striking antithetical image, she likens her lover to both a hideous monster, with snakes for hair, and to the god of war:

> Though he be painted one way like a Gorgon,
> The other way's a Mars.   *(lines 118–19)*

The opposition of 'Gorgon' and 'Mars' epitomises the play's preoccupation with contradiction, and symbolises Cleopatra's character as much as Antony's. The complexities of her character emerge again in the parting command she delivers, that Alexas also find out just how tall Octavia is: the wish to know such seemingly trivial information is simply one small part of Cleopatra's infinite variety.

Act 2 Scene 6

The play returns to Roman politics as Pompey faces the Triumvirate near Misena. The opening stage direction 'with soldiers marching' makes it clear that the two sides have come to fight, but Pompey wishes to talk first and Caesar agrees. Caesar asks Pompey if he will agree to peace terms to avoid bloodshed. In response, Pompey uses carefully measured language to state his case for taking up arms. He seeks revenge for the murder of his father, Pompey the Great, just as Antony and Caesar had avenged the murder of Julius Caesar (who had been responsible for the assassination of Pompey the Great – details of the power struggle leading up to this present confrontation between Pompey and the Triumvirate are given on page 5).

War seems to threaten as Antony makes light of the power of Pompey's navy, and boasts that the Triumvirate's land army far exceeds his. Pompey deflects Antony's brag into a criticism that Antony stole his father's house. Pompey turns it into a joke at Antony's expense, calling him a cuckoo in the nest, but then airily allows Antony to keep the stolen property. The gesture seems to signal an intention to compromise, and the three triumvirs again invite Pompey to respond to the peace terms they offer. Pompey accepts but makes another jibe at Antony, who has not acknowledged the kindness Pompey extended to Antony's mother. Antony immediately offers his 'liberal thanks' for the debt he owes for that courtesy, and the two men shake hands. The threat of war has been avoided, and Antony thanks Pompey for another service he has rendered. His military challenge has drawn Antony away from the seductive pleasures of Egypt and reincorporated him into the military and political duties he owes to Rome:

> The beds i'th'East are soft; and thanks to you,
> That called me timelier than my purpose hither,
> For I have gained by't.   *(lines 50–2)*

The atmosphere seems friendly as Pompey asks for the treaty to be signed before they all feast together. But friction seems likely as Pompey tactlessly talks of Julius Caesar, Cleopatra's former lover. Enobarbus diverts attention to the prospect of four feasts ahead, and he and Pompey express respect for each other. Pompey invites everyone to entertainment on his galley, and the stage empties, leaving the two seasoned war veterans, Enobarbus and Menas, to comment on what has happened.

Menas makes it plain that he thinks Pompey has made a mistake in agreeing to the peace treaty. He and Enobarbus praise each other's fighting skills and shake hands. As they do so, Menas' words provide a cynical comment on the handshakes that Pompey exchanged with Antony:

> All men's faces are true, whatsome'er their hands are.
>
> *(line 99)*

He clearly implies that the temperaments of the triumvirs and Pompey will ensure conflict, even if they have shaken hands. His words prompt Enobarbus to remark, equally cynically, that all women are similarly false. After briefly agreeing that they would prefer to have fought rather than feasted, both men comment sceptically on Antony's marriage to Octavia. They recognise the *realpolitik* that lies behind the arranged marriage and predict conflict between Antony and Caesar when Antony tires of Octavia. Enobarbus uses one of the play's many images of food and eating to forecast what will happen:

> He will to his Egyptian dish again.   *(line 123)*

The tone of the conversation has been one of disillusioned realism. Enobarbus and Menas are clear-sighted about the political deviousness that has cobbled together the peace agreement with Pompey, arranged Antony's marriage, and will eventually destroy the Triumvirate. Antony's infatuation with Cleopatra will be the catalyst that will provoke open conflict between him and Caesar.

Act 2 Scene 7

On board Pompey's galley, servants comment on Lepidus' drunkenness. It is a brief episode to open the scene and it gives the viewpoint of the common people on one of the three great rulers of the world. But Shakespeare ensures that their sceptical comments about Lepidus reflect also on the false unity that the preceding scene presented: Lepidus' appearance, like a star that cannot keep its orbit ('sphere'), or like a face with empty eye sockets, echoes the self-interest and hollowness that underlie the political arrangements the audience has witnessed.

The world leaders enter, with Antony in the middle of a conversation with Caesar. The befuddled Lepidus interrupts, drunkenly showing off his knowledge that the Nile mud breeds snakes and crocodiles (a common belief in Shakespeare's time). Shakespeare gives the tipsy Lepidus plenty of sibilants to slur ('strange serpents', 'Ptolemies' pyramises', etc.). Lepidus is plied with more drink, and Antony ridicules him as he gives a straight-faced but meaningless description of the crocodile. In performance it can be wonderfully comic as Lepidus marvels at what he hears, failing to see its empty circularity, or that he is the butt of the joke.

Alongside the comedy, however, sinister political plotting is taking place. Menas constantly badgers Pompey for a private word and, at last, Pompey agrees. Menas' plan is to make Pompey lord of all the world by cutting the throats of Antony, Caesar and Lepidus. Pompey immediately forbids such action, claiming he puts honour before personal profit. But his attitude is deeply ambivalent, and reveals again the cynical power politics that permeate the play. He twice comments that if Menas had killed the triumvirs without his knowledge, he (Menas) would have deserved praise.

Pompey's uneasy reprimands betray his 'honour', revealing it to be as empty as Antony's definition of the crocodile, mere words. Menas decides to leave Pompey for missing the opportunity to seize power. He turns to drinking with his newfound ally, Enobarbus, who jokes about the strength of the servant who carries off the drink-sodden Lepidus: 'A bears / The third part of the world' on his shoulders.

The feast quickly descends into drunken revelry, plummeting into an imitation of the 'Egyptian Bacchanals' Antony had so much enjoyed in Alexandria with Cleopatra. Enobarbus leads the company in riotous dancing as they stamp out the rhythm of a song. In performance, the heady, excessive, chaotic, yet rhythmic celebrations can be a thrilling spectacle. But every production carefully works out how the puritanical Caesar behaves. Sometimes he joins in awkwardly and with evident discomfort. In other productions he deliberately stands apart, refusing to participate. However a production chooses to present him, his words make his attitude clear:

> Our graver business
> Frowns at this levity. Gentle lords, let's part;
> You see we have burnt our cheeks. Strong Enobarb
> Is weaker than the wine, and mine own tongue
> Splits what it speaks. The wild disguise hath almost
> Anticked us all.   *(lines 114–19)*

As the world leaders make their unsteady way ashore, Menas orders a military salute of drums, and he and Enobarbus cheer as they look forward to continuing their drinking in Menas' cabin. But two modern productions ended the scene with the murder of Pompey, an action unjustified by the text. In one, he was strangled by Caesar's men; in another, he was stabbed by Enobarbus.

Act 2: Critical review

The politics of the play develop rapidly throughout Act 2. In Scene 1, Pompey prepares for war with the Triumvirate. Scene 2 is much concerned with the power struggles within the Roman empire. Antony and Caesar seem to resolve their differences through the marriage of Octavia, Caesar's sister, to Antony. The final episode of the scene, in which Enobarbus describes Cleopatra, undermines the patched-up alliance of the two world leaders, because it forecasts that Antony will be unable to break free of Cleopatra's spell.

By putting the exotic description of Cleopatra into Enobarbus' mouth, Shakespeare intensifies her sensual appeal. Enobarbus is the play's sardonic commentator: plain, blunt and sceptical. Here, his lyrical, admiring praise of Cleopatra stands in sharp contrast to his familiar style, giving the description extraordinary poetic power in its imaginative richness. It shows that the chaste Octavia cannot compete with the beguiling queen. Cleopatra's 'infinite variety', which makes 'defect perfection', will inexorably lure Antony back to Egypt. There his pleasure lies.

Scene 5 displays the defective aspects of Cleopatra's 'variety'. Shakespeare exploits all the dramatic potential of the tradition that the messenger who brings bad news to tyrants suffers for it. The episode is both comic and serious in performance, as the messenger, fearing punishment, delays telling Cleopatra that Antony is married, and as Cleopatra matches her hyperbolic language with equally extreme behaviour.

Cleopatra's capacity for self-delusion is evident as she persists in believing Antony is not married, asking again and again for the messenger to deny the news. Modern criticism and productions acknowledge the absurd humour that Shakespeare's text contains, with Cleopatra awesomely and hilariously out of control.

The act closes, as it began, with Pompey. Peace seems to have been patched up, but the *realpolitik* of the Roman world surfaces in Menas' offer to cut the throats of the triumvirs, even as they enjoy Pompey's hospitality. Pompey's seemingly honourable refusal to sanction the murders is ironically undercut by his regret: if only Menas had committed the murders without his knowledge!

Act 3 Scene 1

The contrast with the preceding scene is starkly ironic. On Pompey's galley, Antony, master of one third of the world, had drunkenly revelled. Here, on the plains of Syria, the serious business of war is being conducted by his subordinate. Antony had dispatched Ventidius to subdue the rebellion of the Parthians, and Scene 1 shows him triumphant. He has slain the son of the rebel leader, so exacting vengeance for the killing of the Roman consul, Crassus (see page 5). Now Silius urges Ventidius on to fresh victories, but Ventidius refuses, all too aware of the dangers for him that such victories would create. He knows that to be too successful would incur Antony's displeasure.

Ventidius reminds Silius of important lessons to learn for survival in Rome's fiercely competitive political and military climate. First, don't acquire fame greater than your master's. Second, all great victories are won not by Rome's rulers, Antony and Caesar, but by the professional commanders under them. Third, remember Antony's lieutenant Sossius, who won military fame, but lost favour as a result. So don't become your 'captain's captain': it is better to lose rather than to win a victory which 'darkens' your reputation with your superior. To put it colloquially, Ventidius is saying, 'Roman generals don't like subordinates who get too big for their boots'.

Ventidius therefore proposes to write 'humbly' to Antony to tell him that victory over the Parthians has been achieved 'in his name', with 'his banners' and 'his well-paid ranks'. Shakespeare is exposing the self-interested reality that lies behind the reputation of Antony as a mighty war leader.

Act 3 Scene 2

The scene begins with Agrippa and Enobarbus mocking Lepidus. They comment on his terrible hangover, calling it 'green-sickness', a form of anaemia supposed to afflict love-sick girls. The two men mimic how Lepidus flatters Antony and Caesar: one he 'loves', the other he 'adores' and he praises them variously as 'Jupiter', 'The god of Jupiter', 'the nonpareil', the 'Arabian bird'. Enobarbus mercilessly ridicules Lepidus' exaggeratedly ingratiating attitude to his fellow triumvirs, and ends with a cynical image of Lepidus as the beetle that feeds on dung ('shards' – though this word can also mean 'wings'):

> They are his shards, and he their beetle.　　　　　*(line 20)*

The image is a satirical preparation for the entrance of the triumvirs. The rest of the scene concerns the parting of Caesar and Octavia. His words of farewell are much concerned with his own reputation and dignity, and he asks Antony to treat his sister well, or their newly-formed alliance will surely falter. Antony bridles at the hint of mistrust in Caesar's words, and assures him he will not find 'the least cause / For what you seem to fear'. Octavia weeps, and as she whispers in Caesar's ear, Antony acknowledges that she is pulled by powerful currents of emotion between himself and her brother, comparing her to

>   the swansdown feather,
> That stands upon the swell at the full of tide,
> And neither way inclines   *(lines 48–50)*

Enobarbus and Agrippa wonder if Caesar will weep, and in cynical asides to each other express doubts about their leaders' sincerity. Weeping was not what a real man would do; even Antony had wept at Julius Caesar's death. Enobarbus sarcastically adds, 'Believe't, till I wept too'. The scene ends with Antony embracing Caesar, and with Caesar's poignant farewell to his sister, 'Adieu. Be happy!' For the audience, who know the falsity of Antony's protestation of trustworthiness and show of love, this parting scene is full of irony. They know he intends to abandon his marriage of convenience and return to Cleopatra.

Act 3 Scene 3

In Alexandria, Cleopatra is determined to question the messenger about Octavia. The scene works very effectively on stage, full of humour as Cleopatra reveals her obsession with her appearance (Charmian feeding her vanity) and the fearful messenger strives to give Cleopatra the answers she wants to hear.

Alexas tells Cleopatra of the messenger's fear, adding that even Herod (noted for his fierceness) would not dare to look upon her when she is angry. Cleopatra extravagantly claims she will have Herod's head (Antony had actually had a Jewish king beheaded) and begins to interrogate the messenger. In performance, Charmian has sometimes signalled to the messenger what answers to give; at other times the messenger goes through agonies as he tries to work out the answers that will excuse him punishment. Cleopatra is increasingly pleased with what she hears, certain that Antony cannot possibly like Octavia long. Her waspish judgement of Octavia's voice and height usually evokes much audience laughter:

> ... Dull of tongue, and dwarfish. *(line 16)*

She demands to know how Octavia walks, ominously reminding the messenger of her own 'majesty'. He, partly apprehensive, and partly prompted by his success so far, offers an outrageous description: 'She creeps'. Cleopatra, encouraged by Charmian, praises his 'good judgement' and is delighted by the news that Octavia is a widow. She invites Charmian to join in her scorn: 'Widow? Charmian, hark.' But, in an intensely comic moment, the atmosphere freezes over as the messenger reports that Octavia is 30. Cleopatra is 38, and in performance there is often a long pause, filled with audience laughter, as Cleopatra struggles to control her shattered emotions and the messenger realises with horror that he has said exactly the wrong thing. Significantly, Shakespeare gives Cleopatra no response to the depressing news that her rival is younger than herself, and actors invent all kinds of stage business to fill the silence (one Charmian fainted clean away).

Cleopatra changes the subject, and the messenger is relieved that he can report (or invent) that Octavia's face is round, she has brown hair and a low forehead. All this pleases Cleopatra, restoring her good humour. She rewards the messenger with gold and half apologises for her earlier mistreatment of him. He leaves, greatly relieved, and Charmian continues to butter up her mistress, echoing Cleopatra's self-admiring praise of the messenger for recognising her true majesty (Charmian's phrase 'Isis else defend' means in effect 'I should think so!'):

CLEOPATRA The man hath seen some majesty, and should know.
CHARMIAN Hath he seen majesty? Isis else defend,
    And serving you so long! *(lines 41–3)*

Act 3 Scene 4

In Athens, Antony complains to Octavia about Caesar's conduct. Shakespeare skilfully begins the scene in the middle of a conversation,

'Nay, nay, Octavia, not only that', which helps create the sense of increasingly strained relationships between Antony and Caesar, and between Antony and his wife. The audience senses a build-up of tension and the continuation of an argument. Antony is angry that Caesar has declared war again on Pompey, spoken insultingly about Antony himself ('scantly of me'), coldly credited his honour, and praised him only grudgingly between clenched teeth. Octavia tries to calm his festering resentment, and feels herself inescapably trapped between her two conflicting loyalties:

> Husband win, win brother,
> Prays and destroys the prayer; no midway
> 'Twixt these extremes at all.   *(lines 18–20)*

Antony talks much of his honour: 'If I lose mine honour, / I lose myself' – a sentiment which must surely prompt the audience to question his sincerity and whether he really knows himself. He has, after all, already decided to desert Octavia. He asks Octavia, as she had requested, to go to Caesar as a go-between to negotiate a reconcilement. This again puts Antony's moral character into question as it seems rather like a convenient way to rid himself of her. His intention to raise a mighty army against Caesar more truly indicates his intentions, because it suggests he knows conflict with Rome will be inevitable when he returns to Cleopatra. Octavia's vision of the world-shattering nature of such a conflict is terrifying:

> Wars 'twixt you twain would be
> As if the world should cleave, and that slain men
> Should solder up the rift.   *(lines 30–2)*

Act 3 Scene 5

This short scene between Enobarbus and Eros provides information about the rapidly worsening political situation. Eros confirms the news of Caesar's war against Pompey, and reveals that Caesar has arrested Lepidus, who awaits death in prison. Only Antony and Caesar now rule. That news prompts Enobarbus to turn Octavia's image (in the previous scene) of the consequences of war between the rivals into a grotesque picture of a pair of jaws chewing up the entire world:

Then, world, thou hast a pair of chaps, no more;
And throw between them all the food thou hast,
They'll grind the one the other. *(lines 11–13)*

Enobarbus' image that an all-devouring war is inevitable is confirmed by the further news that Pompey has been murdered and that Antony's navy is ready for battle.

Act 3 Scene 6

Just as Antony had complained about Caesar in Scene 4, now Caesar catalogues his grievances against Antony. He has contemptuously and arrogantly challenged Rome in the most public fashion. In the market-place in Alexandria, seated with Cleopatra on golden thrones, and surrounded by their children, Antony displayed his imperial power. He made Cleopatra queen of vast regions of the Roman empire, and gave kingdoms, provinces and islands to their sons. It is interesting that Shakespeare chose to report, rather than to dramatise, this lavish pageant of power on display, but the 1992 Royal Shakespeare Company production did enact it; as Caesar indignantly described the ceremony of luxurious excess, it was acted out at the back of the stage in spectacular dumb-show.

Caesar's anger at this insult to his political power is compounded by the fact that Caesarion, the child who Julius Caesar had fathered with Cleopatra ('whom they call my father's son'), was present at the ceremony: Caesar's puritanical mind is outraged by the thought. He has already informed the people of Rome of Antony's conduct, and now adds further charges: Antony has accused Caesar of not giving him part of Sicily (seized from the vanquished Pompey) and of detaining Lepidus at his (Antony's) expense. Caesar briefly sets out the exchange of territories he might negotiate, but his response to Maecenas' comment shows any negotiation is a sham and that Caesar is set upon military action:

MAECENAS He'll never yield to that.
CAESAR Nor must not then be yielded to in this. *(lines 38–9)*

The entry of Octavia with a few attendants seals Caesar's determination for war. Instead of brotherly feeling, his reaction is one of outrage that his own dignity and honour has been offended.

Caesar's sister should always be accompanied by a vast army and elaborate ceremony, but she has come like 'A market maid to Rome'. The need for public display of power weighs more heavily with Caesar than personal affection for his sister. She has 'prevented / The ostentation of our love, which, left unshown, / Is often left unloved' (she has prevented Caesar from putting on the elaborate public ceremony of welcome which is needed to ensure the continued loyalty of the people). This accusation reveals both Caesar's personal coldness and his total preoccupation with the political consequences of any action.

Octavia explains that she has come of her own free will, and that Antony approves of her visit. Caesar cynically, but realistically, identifies Antony's motive in permitting Octavia to leave: his lust for Cleopatra. Octavia tries to defend Antony, but Caesar quickly, even brutally, reveals how her husband has betrayed her and himself:

> Cleopatra
> Hath nodded him to her. He hath given his empire
> Up to a whore, who now are levying
> The kings o'th'earth for war. *(lines 67–70)*

Octavia despairs, 'Ay me most wretched', recognising she is irrevocably trapped between a warring brother and husband. Caesar offers some comfort, but again sets his reassurance in the context of public affairs. Her personal grief must be overridden by the 'strong necessities' of the time: political and military considerations. Destiny itself will bring Caesar victory. At last Caesar seems to express personal concern for Octavia, but he continues to think of himself as the agent of the gods who will see that justice is done.

Maecenas assures Octavia that everyone in Rome loves and pities her, and condemns 'th'adulterous Antony' and his 'trull' (prostitute), Cleopatra. Caesar confirms what Maecenas claims, and ends the scene with 'My dear'st sister!', words that every actor playing Caesar has to decide whether to accompany with an action of some kind. Some have embraced Octavia warmly; others have shown that physical contact and a display of emotion is abhorrent to Caesar's cold and calculating character. He has, after all, used his sister as a bargaining counter to ensure his political power.

Act 3 Scene 7

This scene and the next three are set near Actium, where the decisive sea battle will be fought. Cleopatra and Enobarbus are in the middle of a heated argument, and the veteran soldier speaks with none of the respect due to a queen. He is convinced that the battlefield is no place for a woman, and that her presence will merely distract Antony. He uses a blatantly sexual image: that to have stallions and mares serving together in war invites disaster, as the stallions will only be interested in copulating. Strangely, the sexually aware Cleopatra does not seem to understand the image ('What is't you say?') but in performance the line can be spoken with pretended shock.

Enobarbus persists, saying that in Rome, Antony, already criticised for frivolity, is mocked for handing over his command to women and a eunuch. Cleopatra is unmoved, and hyperbolically dismisses the rumour: 'Sink Rome, and their tongues rot / That speak against us!' She is determined to fight in the coming battle. Antony enters, wondering at the speed with which Caesar has moved to be so threateningly close. His words prompt a caustic comment from Cleopatra on his own lack of preparation:

> Celerity is never more admired
> Than by the negligent.   *(lines 24–5)*

Antony accepts the rebuke and orders the fight to take place at sea. Cleopatra approves the decision, but Canidius and Enobarbus are dismayed. Enobarbus mocks Antony's reason, 'For that he dares us to't', reminding Antony that Caesar has ignored a similar dare to single combat offered by Antony. The seasoned soldier lists sound reasons for not fighting at sea, but Antony rejects his advice. In spite of Enobarbus' insistence that his land forces are far superior, Antony determines on a sea battle. Cleopatra backs him, boasting her sixty ships are better than Caesar's.

More ominous news arrives, and again Antony seems bemused by Caesar's swift and effective generalship. He prepares to leave, flatteringly calling Cleopatra 'my Thetis' (sea-nymph), but a soldier delays him, delivering a warning not to fight by sea. The soldier's style of speech is archaic, rather like a formal chorus, and Shakespeare seems to be using him as a symbolic figure, a supernatural omen of coming disaster. But again Antony is unmoved and merely waves him away, then leaves. The soldier and Canidius agree on the wisdom of fighting on land, and Canidius disgustedly pinpoints the source of Antony's ill-judgement:

> our leader's led,
> And we are women's men.   *(lines 69–70)*

The scene ends with another expression of amazement at the speed with which Caesar has conducted his campaign. Shakespeare is building up the difference between the two leaders, and it is significant that Antony is three times referred to as 'emperor' in the same scene that shows him beginning to lose the military acumen he once possessed, thus highlighting the height from which this once all-powerful joint master of the world will fall.

Act 3 Scenes 8, 9 and 10

Scenes 8 and 9 show Caesar and Antony preparing their forces for the coming sea battle. Caesar has obviously meticulously planned his strategy, whilst Antony proposes to act when he discovers the size of Caesar's navy.

Scene 10 begins with a direction for the two armies to march over the stage, after which *'the noise of a sea fight'* is heard. In Shakespeare's time, drums, trumpets and pipes, together with confused shouting, would probably have been used for sound effects, and many scholars argue that cannonfire would also have been used (the Globe Theatre was burnt down by a fire caused by a cannon in a performance of *King Henry VIII*). In modern performances, the battle is also fought off stage with more sophisticated effects, but in Victorian times some productions presented the battle as a lavish stage spectacle (see pages 104–5).

Enobarbus' anguished words immediately reveal that Antony has disastrously lost the battle because of the flight of Cleopatra's flagship and all her fleet:

> Naught, naught, all naught! I can behold no longer.
> Th'Antoniad, the Egyptian admiral,
> With all their sixty, fly and turn the rudder.
> To see't mine eyes are blasted.   *(lines 1–4)*

Scarus confirms the defeat, and his image lays the responsibility squarely on the mutual infatuation of Antony and Cleopatra: 'We have kissed away / Kingdoms and provinces.' He likens the Roman forces to men infected with the plague ('tokened pestilence' = 'plague sore', a sign of imminent death). He curses Cleopatra: 'Yon ribaudred nag of Egypt – / Whom leprosy o'ertake!' No one is quite sure what Shakespeare meant by 'ribaudred nag'; it has been variously interpreted as meaning 'whore', 'foul, useless horse', 'be-ribboned woman', 'obscene slut', 'abominable female', and many other derogatory terms. Scarus continues his denunciation of Cleopatra, likening her flight to that of a maddened cow stung by a gadfly ('breeze'):

> The breeze upon her, like a cow in June,
> Hoists sail and flies. *(lines 14–15)*

Enobarbus is sickened by what he has seen, and Scarus provides yet another striking image which shows that the defeat was not only a disaster for Antony, but deeply shaming for him. He abandoned the battle and abjectly followed Cleopatra, totally governed by his lust for her:

> Claps on his sea wing, and, like a doting mallard,
> Leaving the fight in height, flies after her.
> I never saw an action of such shame. *(lines 19–21)*

Scarus is incensed that the virtues of 'Experience, manhood, honour' have all been violated. Canidius confirms the battle has been completely lost, and takes Antony's desertion as a model for his own conduct: he will take his legions and cavalry and join forces with Caesar. But Enobarbus, though doubting his own judgement, decides to remain loyal to the disgraced Antony.

Act 3 Scene 11

Antony's shame at what he has done is undisguised. He has not merely been defeated in battle, but has behaved dishonourably in full view of his troops. Feeling ruined and degraded, he expresses his shame in the image of a traveller who has been overtaken by darkness and loses all sense of direction:

> I am so lated in the world that I
> Have lost my way for ever. *(lines 3–4)*

In his shame, he offers his treasure ship to his friends and tells them to make their peace with Caesar. It is a gesture which reveals both his generosity and his present sense of personal worthlessness, although some critics have interpreted it as an act of self-dramatisation, resembling Cleopatra's instinct to dramatise whatever situation she finds herself in. The way in which he then rebukes himself, thinking of his growing age, his fear and his infatuation, is certainly self-dramatic:

> My very hairs do mutiny, for the white
> Reprove the brown for rashness, and they them
> For fear and doting. *(lines 13–15)*

He sits down and falls into such self-absorption, brooding on his defeat and dishonour, that he fails to notice Cleopatra entering with her women and Eros. She too is distracted, unwilling or unable to speak directly to Antony. Shakespeare provides a stage picture of the two lovers utterly apart, each temporarily lost in their own feelings of distress and inadequacy (vividly portrayed in the 1974 television production). Antony is obsessed with thoughts of Caesar, who had played such a minor role at Philippi when they defeated Brutus and Cassius (see *Julius Caesar* Act 5). At that time, Caesar relied totally on his officers and had no battle experience:

> He alone
> Dealt on lieutenantry, and no practice had
> In the brave squares of war. *(lines 38–40)*

'Yet now –' continues Antony, obviously wondering how Caesar has become such an effective general, but he does not complete his thought. Eros unsuccessfully attempts four times to draw Antony's attention to Cleopatra, but Antony, preoccupied with his loss of reputation as a result of his 'most unnoble swerving', ignores him. Only on Eros' fifth attempt does Antony respond, and he reproaches Cleopatra, holding her responsible for his shame and the ruin of his honour:

> O, whither hast thou led me, Egypt? See
> How I convey my shame out of thine eyes
> By looking back what I have left behind
> 'Stroyed in dishonour. *(lines 50–3)*

Cleopatra begs his forgiveness for fleeing the battle, but she places some of the responsibility back on Antony: 'I little thought / You would have followed.' Antony continues to accuse her, saying twice that she well knew he was utterly in her thrall, and would follow whatever she did, unable to resist. She totally commands his heart and his spirit, and not even 'the bidding of the gods' has power against her spell. Antony must now plead humbly to the young Caesar. Whereas once he 'With half the bulk o'th'world played as I pleased, / Making and marring fortunes', she has now weakened him utterly by love. Again Cleopatra begs pardon, and now Antony grants it, asking her for a kiss, which he says will repay all he has lost. His moods swing violently. At one moment he declares he is 'full of lead', at the next, in another gesture of self-dramatisation, he calls for wine and food, and scorns the blows that Fortune has inflicted on him. But the true weakness of his position is conveyed in his brief statement that he has sent his schoolmaster as his ambassador to Caesar. The man who once commanded kings now has only a humble servant to plead for him.

Act 3 Scene 12

Scene 12 underlines the loss of Antony's power as the schoolmaster arrives at Caesar's camp and is described by Dolabella as 'so poor a pinion' (feather) of Antony's wing. Caesar brusquely rejects Antony's plea to live 'A private man in Athens', but says he will accept Cleopatra's submission and allow her to reign in Egypt provided she exile or execute Antony. He peremptorily dismisses the schoolmaster, granting him safe conduct through the Roman lines. Caesar has clearly seen signs of a split between Antony and Cleopatra, and intends to exploit it to the utmost. He dispatches the smooth-tongued Thidias to Cleopatra with instructions to 'win' her from Antony.

Thidias leaves, with orders to 'Try thy cunning' on Cleopatra and to observe how Antony is coping with his disgrace. In the next scene, Caesar's messenger will be treated very differently from the way Antony's schoolmaster was received in this scene.

Act 3 Scene 13

Cleopatra is offered no comfort when she asks, 'What shall we do, Enobarbus?' He replies laconically, 'Think, and die.' His bleak advice sets the tone for this scene, which will portray Antony's further disintegration. Enobarbus blames Antony for the defeat at Actium: his sexual passion overmastered his reason and military judgement. As Enobarbus delivers his shrewd appraisal, Antony enters and informs Cleopatra of Caesar's decision: if she sends Antony's head to Caesar, he will grant all she desires. Antony orders the schoolmaster to return to Caesar, insult his youth and leadership, and dare him to personal combat with Antony. It is an absurdly quixotic challenge, and Enobarbus comments caustically on its unrealistic foolishness:

> Yes, like enough, high-battled Caesar will
> Unstate his happiness and be staged to th'show
> Against a sworder!   *(lines 29–31)*

For Enobarbus, this challenge is a sign of Antony's failing judgement. He begins to question the wisdom of his own loyalty to Antony, but decides to stay because faithfulness to a fallen master should earn a loyal servant an honourable mention in history ('a place i'th'story'). He watches as Cleopatra receives Thidias, and becomes suspicious as she agrees with Caesar's judgement that she acted out of fear of Antony, not love for him. Thinking she is about to betray Antony, Enobarbus leaves to inform his master. Enobarbus has taken Cleopatra's words at face value, but in performance her response to Thidias may be played as ironic, even mocking.

Thidias continues his diplomatic flattery of Cleopatra, assuring her of Caesar's friendship if she abandons Antony and submits to his overlordship. Cleopatra agrees to place herself and Egypt under Caesar's dominion (but significantly says nothing of Antony). Thidias, praising her wisdom, kisses her hand. The 1974 television production added an erotic touch by having Thidias sit on Cleopatra's bed, kissing her hand sensually. She seems flattered by his attention, recalling how Julius Caesar had similarly kissed her hand; but Antony, entering with Enobarbus, is maddened by what he sees. His anger is compounded by Thidias' confident manner, Cleopatra's apparent faithlessness, and the slowness with which his servants respond to his calls. He rages, 'Authority melts from me', but when his servants at last appear, he issues an order that shows his 'Authority' has dwindled to sadistic resentment:

> Take hence this jack and whip him.   *(line 95)*

The contrast with Caesar's cold but courteous treatment of his own ambassador is stark. Thidias' punishment echoes, in crueller form, the beating that Cleopatra inflicted on the hapless messenger who brought her news of Antony's marriage. Enobarbus' sardonic aside reveals not only the dangerous liberty Thidias took with Cleopatra's hand, but aptly portrays Antony's condition:

> 'Tis better playing with a lion's whelp
> Than with an old one dying.   *(lines 96–7)*

Antony turns his anger on Cleopatra: 'You were half blasted ere I knew you.' He calls her a 'boggler' (faithless whore), and curses himself for not seeing the truth earlier. In an outburst of offended masculine bile, using unpleasant images of food, he expresses his disgust:

> I found you as a morsel cold upon
> Dead Caesar's trencher; nay, you were a fragment
> Of Cneius Pompey's   *(lines 119–21)*

Antony rages on, all dignity lost. He questions how Cleopatra could allow a mere servant to kiss the hand that had pledged love to him (for Antony's comparison of himself to a bull of Basan, see page 74). When the whipped Thidias is brought in, Antony humiliates him further, and sends him back to Caesar with a message that is yet another indication of Antony's moral decline: Caesar may similarly whip, or hang, or torture Antony's own servant. It is the perverted tit-for-tat challenge of a petty tyrant, a measure of how far Antony has fallen. As he begins to recover his composure, he uses a memorable image that blames his downfall on Cleopatra (she is the 'terrene moon', an earthly goddess):

> Alack, our terrene moon is now eclipsed,
> And it portends alone the fall of Antony.   *(lines 157–8)*

Cleopatra at last gets her chance to speak, and her impassioned and hyperbolic declaration of love works its instant magic on Antony. His rage evaporates, he accepts her faithfulness ('I am satisfied'), and he prepares to fight Caesar once more. His confidence and hope return as he assesses his military resources and promises to return victorious from battle. Full of bravado, he determines to 'send to darkness all that stop me'. But before the coming battle, he and Cleopatra must enjoy one of their extravagant celebrations:

> Let's have one other gaudy night. Call to me
> All my sad captains. Fill our bowls once more;
> Let's mock the midnight bell.   *(lines 187–9)*

Vowing that the next time he fights he will 'make Death love me', Antony leaves with Cleopatra. In one production, he carried her off triumphantly on his shoulders; in another they clasped each other passionately. In contrast, in another production, Cleopatra, unseen by Antony, displayed dejection and fear. Left alone on stage, Enobarbus decides Antony has now lost all judgement, and determines to desert him.

Act 3: Critical review

Act 3 reads like a film script in its kaleidoscopically changing, ever-contrasting locations, moods and actions. Shakespeare displays his mastery of the freedom allowed by the Jacobean stage as one scene flows swiftly into the next. Scene 1 is vital to an understanding of the politics of the play. It shows the vast range of the world that the play embraces, and casts a sceptical eye on the actual achievements of Antony and his fellow triumvirs (their victories are won for them by their subordinates). Ventidius reveals that 'ambition' rather than 'honour' is the driving force of Roman militarism.

The action quickly unfolds. The audience already knows that Antony's politically arranged marriage to Octavia cannot last, and her return to Caesar, with the intention of preventing war with Antony, in fact precipitates it. For Caesar, already incensed by the news that Antony has crowned himself and Cleopatra in glorious splendour, Octavia's humble appearance is an insult to his honour.

Act 3 reveals Caesar's skill as a war leader and Antony's loss of military judgement. Antony is taken aback by Caesar's tactical skill, but, against all good advice, foolishly decides to fight at sea. The battle of Actium, which takes place off stage, is the turning point of the play. Cleopatra's defection is disastrous. Antony follows her, shamefully deserting his own forces. It is an act of cowardice, and Antony's example is morally corrupting. His honour has gone, and his lieutenants begin to desert, following their own self-interest.

Antony's shame is palpable: 'I / Have lost my way for ever'. The abject decline of his fortune is evident in that he has only his schoolmaster to send as ambassador to Caesar. The mission is unsuccessful and, in the act's final scene, his treatment of Thidias, Caesar's messenger, bears witness to his moral decline. Discovering Thidias kissing Cleopatra's hand, he has him savagely whipped and embarks on a bitter tirade of abuse against Cleopatra. But in the ever-changing emotions that characterise the play, Antony forgives Cleopatra, recovers his martial spirit and looks forward to one more 'gaudy night' of celebration before attacking Caesar once more. The loyal Enobarbus, seeing the 'diminution in our captain's brain', resolves he too must defect.

Act 4 Scene 1

In his camp near Alexandria, Caesar is angered that Antony has derisively called him 'boy' and has had Thidias whipped. He scornfully rejects Antony's challenge to personal combat. Maecenas urges Caesar to take advantage of Antony's mad rage: it is a sure sign that he feels like a hunted animal, and will cause his downfall. Caesar commands that preparations be made for tomorrow's fight, 'the last of many battles', in which he will use soldiers who have deserted from Antony. He orders that his troops be feasted (but in a manner that contrasts sharply with Antony's similar order in the preceding scene) and leaves with a contemptuous expression of pity for his enemy: 'Poor Antony!'

Act 4 Scene 2

Antony learns of Caesar's refusal to fight him in personal combat. Determined to fight to the death tomorrow, he orders a 'bounteous' meal tonight. He calls for his personal servants, greets each warmly, thanking them for their loyalty and honesty, and commands them to keep his wine cup well filled tonight and treat him as he was when he was master of the empire. It is an expression of comradeship, but Cleopatra is puzzled by Antony's behaviour. Enobarbus' explanation that it is 'To make his followers weep' seems uncannily plausible as Antony speaks poignantly that this may be the last service his servants will perform for him:

> May be it is the period of your duty.
> Haply you shall not see me more, or if,
> A mangled shadow.   *(lines 26–8)*

Although some critics have seen Antony's words as self-regardingly pathetic and self-consciously dramatic, the servants weep. Enobarbus protests (possibly ironically) that he too is 'onion-eyed'. He appeals to Antony, 'For shame, / Transform us not to women.' His words cause Antony to deny any such intention: he spoke only to comfort, not to sadden his followers. Expressing confidence that he will be victorious tomorrow, Antony orders everyone to supper, where they can drown all brooding thoughts in drink. In spite of his talk of victory, a strong impression of lost hope pervades the scene, suggesting that, for all his bravado, Antony knows he stares defeat in the face.

Act 4 Scene 3

The scene begins with Antony's soldiers preparing for their night watch. They are apprehensive about how tomorrow's battle will go, but one soldier expresses confidence: if their navy succeeds, then the army too will 'stand up'. As the guards settle at their posts, the atmosphere eerily changes with the sound of strange music. Shakespeare introduces an ominous supernatural element into the play as the soldiers strain to listen and make sense of the sounds, which seem to come from the air and under the earth. One soldier thinks it is a good omen, but another interprets it as a melancholy portent of Antony's downfall:

> 'Tis the god Hercules, whom Antony loved,
> Now leaves him.   *(lines 21–2)*

Antony considered Hercules as his patron and model. In this mysterious episode, Shakespeare suggests that Antony's fate may have been decided by the gods: Hercules is abandoning Antony, signifying that his tragic destiny is unavoidable.

Act 4 Scene 4

The ominous tone of Scene 3 is at once ironically challenged by Antony's impatient confidence: he calls for his armour, determined to defy fortune as he prepares for battle. Cleopatra helps Antony to buckle on his armour, and he lovingly laughs at her efforts, poetically describing her as 'The armourer of my heart'. He praises Cleopatra's help, declaring her a more skilful attendant than Eros. He wishes she could see how excellent a warrior he is in battle and, in greeting a soldier who enters, claims he loves war and goes to it with delight. His words appear to imply that the values of love and war are identical.

Antony seems to have regained all his decisiveness and qualities of military leadership. Learning his army is ready and awaits him, he exudes boldness and self-possession as he issues orders, kisses Cleopatra farewell and leaves her 'like a man of steel'. It is an impressive display of self-assurance, and in performance his soldiers are usually visibly cheered and inspired by his example. But Cleopatra's hesitation as she thinks about the battle's outcome restores the note of sinister foreboding that characterised the strange music of the preceding scene:

He goes forth gallantly. That he and Caesar might
Determine this great war in single fight!
Then Antony – but now – Well, on. *(lines 36–8)*

Act 4 Scenes 5 and 6

In Scene 5, Antony admits his fault in not taking the soldier's advice
to fight on land at Actium. He learns of Enobarbus' desertion and
shows his magnanimity in ordering that his friend's treasure be sent
after him. It is a generous, open-hearted gesture, and there is pathos
in how Antony frankly acknowledges why such followers as
Enobarbus have left him:

> O, my fortunes have
> Corrupted honest men. Dispatch. – Enobarbus! *(lines 16–17)*

Enobarbus appears in Scene 6 in the company of Caesar, but he is
a silent onlooker as Caesar orders that Antony is to be taken alive
(doubtless so that he can be displayed as a prisoner in Caesar's
triumphal return to Rome). Caesar anticipates victory and, in words
which had special resonance for Jacobean audiences (see page 77), he
prophesies a time of peace ahead:

> The time of universal peace is near.
> Prove this a prosp'rous day, the three-nooked world
> Shall bear the olive freely. *(lines 5–7)*

It sounds the noblest of aspirations, but Enobarbus also hears what
fate Caesar has in mind for him: the deserters from Antony are to be
placed in the front rank of battle, and so will be the first to be killed. It
is the chilling decision of a cold-hearted general whose 'universal
peace' is to be ruthlessly achieved. Caesar leaves, and Enobarbus
reflects on the fate of other deserters: hanged or distrusted.

Enobarbus' discomfort at his own treachery is increased as he
learns that all his possessions have been sent over and added to by
Antony. He tries to give them to the soldier who has brought the news,
but the soldier refuses and praises Antony: 'Your emperor /
Continues still a Jove.' Antony's generosity leaves Enobarbus guilt-
stricken. The difference between his two masters is all too plain. He
accuses himself of being 'alone the villain of the earth' and sees only
one way out of his shameful disgrace:

> I will go seek
> Some ditch wherein to die. The foul'st best fits
> My latter part of life.   *(lines 38–40)*

Act 4 Scenes 7 and 8

These two scenes depict Antony's unexpected victory. Stage productions carefully work out how any fighting might be staged, but it seems likely that in Shakespeare's time no battle action was shown, because the stage direction 'Alarum' means a call to arms, rather than stage action of combat. However, most modern productions begin both scenes with some kind of hand-to-hand skirmishing. In Scene 7, Agrippa reports that Caesar's forces have retreated before Antony's fierce attacks. Antony appears with the wounded Scarus, bloody but eager to resume the fight, and together with Eros they leave to pursue Caesar's retreating forces.

In performance, Scene 8 flows seamlessly from Scene 7. Antony, exultant, sends a soldier to tell Cleopatra of his victory and vows that tomorrow he will complete the annihilation of Caesar's forces. He thanks his soldiers for their bravery and orders them to tell their wives and friends of their deeds. Riding on the crest of his soaring emotions, he refers to Cleopatra as a magical enchantress ('great fairy') and greets her as his commander who must triumphantly possess his panting heart:

> O thou day o'th'world,
> Chain mine armed neck; leap thou, attire and all,
> Through proof of harness to my heart, and there
> Ride on the pants triumphing!   *(lines 13–16)*

Cleopatra's equally joyous response is expressed with similarly heightened imaginative power:

> Lord of lords,
> O infinite virtue, com'st thou smiling from
> The world's great snare uncaught?   *(lines 16–18)*

Antony boasts he has beaten Caesar back to his camp and, ruefully admitting he is getting old (grey hairs mingle with brown), claims his brain and physical powers still match any younger man's. He commends Scarus and begs Cleopatra to offer her hand for the wounded warrior to kiss as a reward for his godlike bravery. It is a gesture that ironically contrasts with Antony's treatment of Thidias, who also received that favour from the queen. Cleopatra, typically extravant, promises Scarus 'An armour all of gold', and the scene ends with Antony preparing to take Cleopatra's hand and lead the army back in 'a jolly march' through Alexandria, where he hopes for a night of feasting and drinking before tomorrow's battle.

Act 4 Scene 9

The previous scene ended in an ear-splitting fanfare. Scene 9 opens in the quiet of night at Caesar's camp as the sentries talk apprehensively of the coming battle. They are surprised to see Enobarbus entering and decide to overhear what he says. Enobarbus appeals to the moon as 'sovereign mistress of true melancholy': the very deepest despair. He begs her to break his heart for his cruel treachery and acknowledges Antony's generous nature, which makes his treason even worse: 'Nobler than my revolt is infamous'. He begs Antony's forgiveness and dies condemning his own dishonourable conduct:

> But let the world rank me in register
> A master-leaver and a fugitive.
> O Antony! O Antony!   *(lines 21–3)*

Enobarbus' death from shame signifies both the loyalty Antony can inspire and the code of honour which so strictly binds Roman soldiers that disgrace is unbearable. The sentries, unsure whether Enobarbus is dead or asleep, try to wake him. Discovering that 'The hand of death hath raught him', they bear his body away.

Act 4 Scenes 10, 11 and 12

Three scenes give brief flashes of the preparations for the sea battle and the reactions of the generals to the battle. In Scene 10, Antony learns that Caesar's navy has put to sea and decides to do likewise. In Scene 11, Caesar orders his land army to maintain a defensive position. In Scene 12, Antony leaves to observe the sea battle, noise of the encounter is heard, and Scarus broods on the ill omens for Antony: swallows nest in the sails of Cleopatra's ships; the augurers (soothsayers) are unable to predict the outcome; and Antony's volatile mood switches from hope to fear. Scarus' foreboding is confirmed as Antony returns, cursing Cleopatra:

> All is lost!
> This foul Egyptian hath betrayèd me.
> My fleet hath yielded to the foe, and yonder
> They cast their caps up and carouse together
> Like friends long lost. *(lines 9–13)*

He continues to condemn Cleopatra ('Triple-turned whore!' signifies his disgust that she seduced Julius Caesar, Pompey the Great and himself) and vows vengeance on her. He orders Scarus to tell all his followers to disperse and reflects on the ending of his power. He uses memorable images of melting and dissolving to express how support has dwindled away from him:

> The hearts
> That spanieled me at heels, to whom I gave
> Their wishes, do discandy, melt their sweets
> On blossoming Caesar *(lines 20–3)*

The image reflects the fawning servility of spaniel dogs and the Jacobean custom of feeding dogs with sweetmeats during meals. Feeling betrayed, comparing himself to a dying pine tree stripped of its bark, Antony turns his venom again on Cleopatra: 'this false soul of Egypt!' He sees her as a deadly enchantress ('grave charm') and a 'right gipsy' who has utterly betrayed him: 'Beguiled me to the very heart of loss'. Her appearance enrages him further and he orders her away as if she were a witch: 'Ah, thou spell! Avaunt!' Cleopatra asks why he is so enraged, but Antony only unleashes another torrent of abuse, threatening her life, hoping Caesar will display her in triumph to be mocked as a monster by doltish Roman plebeians. His final cruel taunt causes Cleopatra to leave:

> and let
> Patient Octavia plough thy visage up
> With her preparèd nails! *(lines 37–9)*

Antony vows to kill Cleopatra, using a complex image from classical mythology ('The shirt of Nessus . . . horns o'th'moon'). Antony is likening himself to Hercules (Alcides), from whom he claimed to be descended. Nessus the Centaur, mortally wounded by Hercules, gave a shirt soaked in his poisoned blood to Hercules' wife, Deianira, saying it would act as a love charm to win back Hercules' affection. She sent Lichas to give the shirt to Hercules. When he put it on, the poison fatally maddened him and he hurled the innocent Lichas into the sea. Antony, unable to think that he himself bears much responsibility for his downfall, sees himself similarly mortally wounded by Cleopatra, and in his fury intends to destroy both her and himself:

> The witch shall die.
> To the young Roman boy she hath sold me, and I fall
> Under this plot. She dies for't. *(lines 47–9)*

Act 4 Scene 13

Back in her palace, Cleopatra fears Antony's frenzied wrath. She likens him to Telamon (Ajax, an impetuously dangerous Greek hero) and to 'the boar of Thessaly' (a savage animal), foaming at the mouth ('embossed'). Charmian gives Cleopatra fatal advice: she should lock herself in her monument and send word to Antony that she is dead. Cleopatra instantly accepts Charmian's hazardous counsel, but cannot help embellishing it. She orders Mardian to say piteously that her dying word was 'Antony', and adds an instruction that reveals her narcissistic self-regard:

> And bring me how he takes my death. *(line 10)*

Act 4 Scene 14

The previous scenes have switched rapidly from palace to camp, from one part of the battlefield to another. Now the two long final scenes of Act 4 focus closely on the death of Antony. Scene 14 begins with Antony, his violent hysteria gone, reflecting that his whole identity is dissolving like the evening clouds. Sometimes the clouds appear like a bear or lion, a towered city, a rock or a mountain. They might take the form of an animal, but then suddenly all shape is lost:

> That which is now a horse, even with a thought
> The rack dislimns and makes it indistinct
> As water is in water.   *(lines 9–11)*

Just as the cloud mass loses its distinctive outline ('The rack dislimns'), so Antony believes he has lost his 'visible shape': Cleopatra's betrayal has made his heroic selfhood become merely a shifting illusion. He loved her, fought Caesar for her, but she 'Packed cards' with Caesar and played him false. Antony sees no way out other than to kill himself.

Antony is at his most vulnerable, and Mardian's entry compounds Antony's sense of the shame Cleopatra has inflicted on him: 'She has robbed me of my sword.' The eunuch's false report of Cleopatra's suicide, delivered with sentimental embroidering, is the final blow that resolves Antony utterly for death:

> Unarm, Eros. The long day's task is done,
> And we must sleep.   *(lines 35–6)*

As Eros assists his master to remove his armour, Antony speaks of the 'battery' (emotional assaults) he suffers. He strips himself physically ('Bruisèd pieces, go') and mentally of his image as a great warrior, and determines to die so that he can meet Cleopatra in the afterlife. He fantasises about their future romance in the underworld, outshining Dido, Queen of Carthage, and her lover Aeneas, founder of Rome:

> I come, my queen. – Eros! – Stay for me.
> Where souls do couch on flowers, we'll hand in hand,
> And with our spritely port make the ghosts gaze.
> Dido and her Aeneas shall want troops,
> And all the haunt be ours.   *(lines 50–4)*

But Antony's image is unwittingly baleful. In Roman legend, Dido killed herself when Aeneas deserted her to follow his Roman duty, and when they met later in the underworld, Dido scornfully refused to acknowledge him. But Antony feels ashamed that he still lives when Cleopatra's brave death has shown him how to die. He, who had 'Quartered [divided and conquered] the world' and assembled vast fleets of ships, like cities, lacks the courage she has shown by defying

Caesar in death. He orders Eros to kill him, a command which Eros had long ago vowed to obey. But the devoted Eros refuses, and Antony makes a fresh appeal. Is Eros willing to see Antony humiliated in Rome, Caesar's captive, led bound behind his chariot? Eros reluctantly agrees, but asks Antony to turn his face away as he strikes.

There follows a tense and poignant moment of leave-taking. Eros bids his master farewell but, to 'escape the sorrow / Of Antony's death', kills himself. Antony is deeply moved by the nobility of Eros' suicide and takes it as a lesson for his own. His image unites the notions of love and death:

> But I will be
> A bridegroom in my death and run into't
> As to a lover's bed.   *(lines 99–101)*

Antony falls on his sword, but his wound is not immediately fatal. Shakespeare denies Antony the dignity of a successful suicide strike and he is forced to plead with the guards to kill him. All refuse, and Dercetus sees the bungled suicide attempt as his chance to win favour with Caesar. He takes Antony's sword to present to Caesar. Dercetus' act of political opportunism has been interpreted as another rat leaving the sinking ship; and Shakespeare provides yet another cynical and ironic twist to deepen the bathos of Antony's suicide attempt as Diomedes tells Antony the truth, that Cleopatra lives.

'Too late' is Antony's only comment, echoing Diomedes' own words. Knowing he has only a little time to live, Antony orders his sorrowing guards to carry him to Cleopatra at the monument. His command displays the stoicism he feels in the face of death.

Act 4 Scene 15

The staging of the 'monument scene' varies greatly from production to production, but all productions must create a setting in which Cleopatra and her women are 'aloft', so that they can draw up Antony to them. Cleopatra vows she will never leave the monument, and, intent on experiencing the sorrow appropriate to her misfortunes, rejects Charmian's attempt to comfort her. The entry of the guards, carrying the mortally wounded Antony, moves her to express her grief in an apocalyptic image of universal destruction and shadow:

O sun,
Burn the great sphere thou mov'st in; darkling stand
The varying shore o'th'world!   (*lines 10–12*)

Distraught, she orders him to be drawn up to her. He offers
reassurance: not Caesar's bravery, but his own, has vanquished him.
Cleopatra applauds and echoes his confident boast: 'none but Antony
/ Should conquer Antony'. Antony begs death to hold off until he has
kissed Cleopatra. His words cause her momentarily to hesitate, afraid
to come down to him for fear of capture. But she overcomes her fear
and extravagantly claims that she will commit suicide rather than be
seized to be shown in Caesar's triumph and to endure Octavia's
demure gaze. She again orders Charmian and Iras to help her draw
Antony up to her, and half jokes as they lift him, 'Here's sport
indeed!', words which embody both tragic irony and comic bathos.

The women struggle with their heavy burden, and Cleopatra
wishes for the strength of the queen of the gods, 'great Juno's power',
to bring him swiftly to her. At last they succeed and she welcomes him
with a kiss. Antony again exclaims, 'I am dying, Egypt, dying', and
asks for wine. Cleopatra will not let him speak until she has cursed
'the false huswife Fortune', but Antony urges her to seek safety from
Caesar and to trust only Proculeius. Typically, it is advice that will
prove ironically ill-judged in Act 5.

Antony urges Cleopatra not to grieve, but to remember his former
glory when he lived as 'the greatest prince o'th'world, / The noblest'.
The words are appropriate to a tragic hero close to death but, as with
so much of what both Antony and Cleopatra say, they are patently
false. The audience has seen Antony behaving ignobly on many
occasions throughout the play. As so often in their speeches, both
Antony and Cleopatra substitute illusion and hyperbole for truth; but
in the context of this scene and Act 5, their poetic expression is
appropriate to the genre of tragedy and to the view they possess of
themselves as peerless lovers and all-powerful monarchs.

Antony dies, confident that he has achieved a noble death and that
he, not Caesar, has conquered: 'a Roman by a Roman / Valiantly
vanquished'. The grief-stricken Cleopatra seems to rebuke him: how
can she remain behind in a world that his absence makes no better
than a pigsty? In a passage of extraordinary poetic power, she calls
upon her women to witness Antony's death:

> O see, my women:
> The crown o'th'earth doth melt. My lord!
> O, withered is the garland of the war;
> The soldier's pole is fall'n! Young boys and girls
> Are level now with men; the odds is gone,
> And there is nothing left remarkable
> Beneath the visiting moon. *(lines 64–70)*

The complex yet mellifluous imagery is discussed on page 113. Here it will merely be noted that the speech begins with one of the many images of melting that pervade the play, then combines natural and martial imagery in a lament. The image of 'The soldier's pole is fall'n' carries a wealth of possible associations (only one of which is that of a military standard carried before troops into battle). The final two lines suggest that after Antony's death everything in the world is reduced to a dull sameness.

Cleopatra faints and her women desperately try to revive her. When she recovers, she makes what is for Cleopatra a remarkable admission: she identifies herself with all women, even the very humblest, sharing the same feelings:

> No more but e'en a woman, and commanded
> By such poor passion as the maid that milks
> And does the meanest chares. *(lines 78–80)*

Such expression of common humanity gives Cleopatra remarkable dignity in performance. She reproaches the gods for stealing Antony, 'our jewel', and asserts that nothing matters now that he is dead: 'All's but naught'. She determines on death and cheers her women, but reminds them that 'Our lamp is spent'. They will bury Antony then take their own lives 'after the high Roman fashion', making death proud to take them. It is an outstanding display of self-assurance. Even though Cleopatra may be yet again dramatising her situation in her desolation, her words possess dignity and confidence. Her final couplet begins with the women's isolation, but ends with ringing determination:

> Ah, women, women! Come, we have no friend
> But resolution and the briefest end. *(lines 95–6)*

Act 4: Critical review

Once again, Shakespeare creates a kaleidoscope of scenes. The focus constantly changes, but everything works inexorably towards the death of Antony. In Scene 2, Antony's farewell makes his followers weep; in Scene 3, the sentries hear Antony's god Hercules deserting him. In Scene 4, Cleopatra helps Antony buckle on his armour for battle, but in the following scene he hears of Enobarbus' defection. He enjoys a brief victory, but loses the final battle and curses Cleopatra as the cause of his defeat. Her deception, leading him to think her dead, prompts Antony's botched suicide attempt. Learning she lives, he is taken to the monument, where he dies in Cleopatra's arms.

Such a bald description of Antony's decline and death must be supplemented with a summary of key features of the act which embody important themes of the play:

- *Desertion* Antony has already lost many of his followers to Caesar. Now, in Act 4, his guiding spirit, the god Hercules, deserts him, as does his most trusted soldier, Enobarbus. As Antony lies fatally wounded, Dercetus steals his sword and defects, cynically hoping to find favour with Caesar. But Caesar's coldly calculated actions show the fate of deserters: Alexas is hanged, Canidius distrusted, and all other deserters are put in the front rank of battle, to be the first killed.

- *Loyalty* Enobarbus cannot bear the dishonour of his desertion. His loyalty to Antony causes his death from shame. Eros' loyalty also causes his death. He cannot kill his beloved master. Charmian's loyalty to Cleopatra leads her to offer her mistress the fatal advice that causes Antony to attempt suicide.

- *Love* Eros' name (meaning 'love') is threaded through Scene 14, giving constant reminders of the creative and destructive power of love that characterises the play. That power is vividly displayed in the two final scenes: Antony cannot bear to live without Cleopatra, and she, consumed with grief, similarly resolves to die.

- *Change and dissolution* The lovers' volatile emotions reflect their changing political fortunes. Antony feels he loses all identity in defeat: 'As water is in water'. Cleopatra mourns his death in an image of deliquescence: 'The crown o'th'earth doth melt'.

Act 5 Scene 1

At his camp outside Alexandria, Caesar is unaware of Antony's death. He dispatches Dolabella to insist that Antony surrenders; if Antony delays, he will simply appear foolish. The entrance of Dercetus with Antony's sword initially surprises and offends Caesar (in Shakespeare's England it was a treasonable offence to appear in the monarch's presence with a weapon drawn). Dercetus praises Antony, offers to serve Caesar, then plainly delivers his message: 'Antony is dead'. Caesar seems almost to disbelieve the news, and expresses his amazement in language which both echoes the 'world' images of the play and which also recalls the strange and unnatural events that took place in Rome the night before Julius Caesar was murdered (see *Julius Caesar* Act 1 Scene 3, lines 20–35 and Act 2 Scene 2, lines 13–37):

> The breaking of so great a thing should make
> A greater crack. The round world
> Should have shook lions into civil streets
> And citizens to their dens. The death of Antony
> Is not a single doom; in the name lay
> A moiety of the world.   *(lines 14–19)*

Dercetus tells of Antony's suicide and presents the bloodstained sword to Caesar. The sight provokes the watching Roman generals to weep, and each pays tribute to the man who had once ruled half ('A moiety') of the world. Maecenas' shrewd appraisal of Antony aptly identifies his complex nature, his greatness and imperfections combined: 'His taints and honours / Waged equal with him.' Agrippa makes a similarly balanced appraisal, describing Antony as a 'rarer spirit', but, like all men, with faults. Caesar also weeps, seeing a reflection of himself in Antony. His generous tribute to his dead rival stresses their shared purpose and what they had in common as fellow triumvirs.

However, Caesar concludes that their 'stars' were 'Unreconciliable' and so he and Antony were destined to be divided. The messenger from Cleopatra ends talk of Antony as he reports that Cleopatra awaits whatever fate Caesar decrees for her. Caesar promises she will be treated honourably and kindly, but after the messenger leaves, Caesar reveals he has her humiliation in mind. He dispatches Proculeius to ensure Cleopatra does not commit suicide, for he intends that she shall be taken to Rome to be displayed as an everlasting symbol of his triumph. Caesar's steely political will is much in evidence here, and his concern for his public reputation is equally evident in his concern to justify himself even to his own his generals:

> How hardly I was drawn into this war,
> How calm and gentle I proceeded still   *(lines 74–5)*

Caesar, the victor, will write his own version of history.

Act 5 Scene 2

> My desolation does begin to make
> A better life.   *(lines 1–2)*

Cleopatra's opening words suggest she is beginning to recognise the worthlessness of her former glory. She scorns Caesar, saying that he is merely 'Fortune's knave', bound to do her (Fortune's) will. In view of what Caesar has just decided shall be her fate, Cleopatra's assessment of him seems strikingly misjudged. Once again she is declaring things to be as she wishes, deceiving herself about their reality. But Cleopatra has no illusions about what she intends for herself: suicide. Her description of the action of taking one's life is full of complex imagery:

> And it is great
> To do that thing that ends all other deeds,
> Which shackles accidents and bolts up change,
> Which sleeps, and never palates more the dung,
> The beggar's nurse and Caesar's.   *(lines 4–8)*

For Cleopatra, suicide is a noble act ('great'). It means that she will no longer be vulnerable to chance ('accidents') and ageing ('change'); death puts an end to them, and the image she uses is of chaining them up, 'shackles accidents and bolts up change'. Death will grant her sleep and she will never again have to taste the 'dung', the base produce of the earth that gives life to beggar and king alike. Cleopatra's vision is an illusion, but expressed in astounding language, which shores up her determination at this moment to be mistress of her fate and to conquer the misfortunes and sordidness of the earthly world.

Proculeius brings greetings from Caesar. Cleopatra, despite Antony's advice to trust Proculeius, expresses some suspicion of Caesar's messenger: 'I do not greatly care to be deceived'. She sets out her terms: if her son can rule Egypt, she will submit to Caesar. Proculeius assures her of Caesar's generous intentions for her, but his seemingly comforting words are belied as Roman guards break in and seize Cleopatra. She draws her dagger, but Proculeius prevents her from stabbing herself and once more assures her that she is 'Relieved, but not betrayed'. He counsels her not to abuse Caesar's generosity by taking her own life, but to

> Let the world see
> His nobleness well acted, which your death
> Will never let come forth. *(lines 43–5)*

Cleopatra's response is hyperbolically self-dramatic:

> Where art thou, Death?
> Come hither, come! Come, come, and take a queen
> Worth many babes and beggars. *(lines 45–7)*

She continues in the same exaggerated vein, vowing not to eat or drink or sleep: 'This mortal house I'll ruin'. Cleopatra vigorously expresses her festering jealous disdain for Octavia and her fear of being displayed to the 'shouting varletry' in a Roman triumph. Rather than such degrading indignities, she would prefer to die in a ditch in Egypt. Her imagination soars as she lists other deaths she would rather endure before such shaming dishonours:

> Rather on Nilus' mud
> Lay me stark nak'd and let the water-flies
> Blow me into abhorring! Rather make
> My country's high pyramides my gibbet
> And hang me up in chains! *(lines 57–61)*

Proculeius mildly rebukes her for such 'thoughts of horror', assuring her that Caesar's intentions should give her no cause for fear. He promises to carry her reply to Caesar, but she gives him an uncompromising message: 'Say I would die.' Left in the protection of Dolabella, Cleopatra's mood changes. She half jokes that he laughs 'when boys or women tell their dreams'. Dolabella is puzzled, but Cleopatra's intention is to tell of her own dream of Antony. As Dolabella unsuccessfully tries to speak, she declares that she longs to dream again of a man whose face 'was as the heav'ns' and, like the sun and moon, gave light to 'The little O, the earth'. Once again, Cleopatra's imagination takes flight, but in quite a different tone and matter from how she had just extravagantly imagined her death. Her description of Antony continues to portray him as a microcosm of the universe:

> His legs bestrid the ocean; his reared arm
> Crested the world; his voice was propertied
> As all the tunèd spheres, and that to friends;
> But when he meant to quail and shake the orb,
> He was as rattling thunder. For his bounty,
> There was no winter in't; an autumn 'twas
> That grew the more by reaping. His delights
> Were dolphin-like; they showed his back above
> The element they lived in. In his livery
> Walked crowns and crownets; realms and islands were
> As plates dropped from his pocket.   *(lines 81–91)*

Cleopatra's vision of a superhuman Antony endows him with legendary magnificence and munificence: a Colossus, with a voice that was melodious when speaking to friends but awesomely terrible when addressing foes; infinitely generous, and 'dolphin-like', joyously delighting in all worldly pleasures; with kings and princes in his service, and freely bestowing territories. Again, Cleopatra is in a world of illusion, but her fantasy is poignantly and lyrically expressed in an elegiac celebration of Antony. It is a language style which demonstrates that she shares equal tragic status with Antony. Both live, in their minds, in a world far from the commonplace realities of everyday existence. It is a state of mind in which Cleopatra's image of her hero can withstand Dolabella's courteous denial:

CLEOPATRA Think you there was or might be such a man
        As this I dreamt of?
DOLABELLA   Gentle madam, no.   *(lines 92–3)*

Cleopatra accuses Dolabella of lying, but admits that her conception of Antony is beyond any dream. Nature itself cannot compete with fantasy, but Nature's imagination can create a real Antony, a masterpiece, superior to any other imagined version of him. Dolabella acknowledges Cleopatra's grief, and hesitantly reveals what Cleopatra fears: that Caesar intends to lead her in triumph through Rome. Before Cleopatra can respond, Caesar enters and she kneels in submission to him. He promises not to bear resentment for the injuries she has done him and, after Cleopatra confesses to the 'frailties' which have 'often shamed our sex', Caesar promises gentle treatment. But in promising no harm will come to her, he threatens that her children will suffer if she, like Antony, commits suicide.

Cleopatra seems to assent, but, like Caesar, she knows that what they say to each other conceals their real intentions. In the brief episode that follows, Cleopatra's lying is instantly, even comically, revealed as her treasurer Seleucus tells the truth: that she has declared to Caesar only half of her wealth. Cleopatra hysterically accuses Seleucus of ingratitude and threatens him, just as she had abused the messenger who brought her news of Antony's marriage. As Seleucus backs away, fearing she will punish him, she insults him: 'Slave, soulless villain, dog! / O rarely base!' (But it should be noted that some critics have interpreted the Seleucus episode as pre-arranged by Cleopatra as a ruse to trick Caesar into believing that she does not intend to commit suicide.)

Cleopatra tries to excuse herself to Caesar, blaming Seleucus, and saying she kept back some 'lady trifles' as gifts for Livia (Caesar's wife) and Octavia. She again condemns Seleucus who, after a further threat of violence from Cleopatra, is ordered away by Caesar. Her whole speech is probably an act for Caesar's benefit, to preserve her dignity, but she continues to blame the unfortunate treasurer, claiming that as queen she must answer for her servants' faults and so deserves pity. Caesar brushes the problem away, saying Cleopatra may keep all her treasure. He leaves with reassuring words, promising friendship.

Caesar is lying, and Cleopatra knows it. All his soothing words are intended to prevent her suicide so that he can take her in triumph to Rome. She expresses her distrust to her women, 'He words me, girls, he words me', then whispers to Charmian (Shakespeare gives no indication of what she whispers – perhaps some instruction about the suicide to come). Iras' sombre imagery (echoing Antony's 'The long day's task is done, / And we must sleep') poetically expresses what will be the women's fate:

> Finish, good lady. The bright day is done,
> And we are for the dark. *(lines 192–3)*

Dolabella returns to confirm Cleopatra's fears about Caesar's deceit: she and her children are to be taken to Rome. Cleopatra knows just what that means and describes the humiliation she and her women will suffer if led in Caesar's triumphal parade: the foul breath of workmen ('Mechanic slaves') will choke them, insolent Roman officials ('lictors') will paw them as if they were prostitutes, and contemptible ('scald') ballad-makers will sing obscene songs about them. Cleopatra paints a vivid picture of the ribald shows that will parody her and Antony:

> The quick comedians
> Extemporally will stage us and present
> Our Alexandrian revels; Antony
> Shall be brought drunken forth, and I shall see
> Some squeaking Cleopatra boy my greatness
> I'th'posture of a whore. *(lines 215–20)*

Iras vows to tear out her eyes rather than witness the sight Cleopatra describes. Cleopatra approves and, intent on death, orders her women to fetch 'My best attires' to dress her like a queen. She declares her death will be a re-enactment of her first meeting with Antony:

> I am again for Cydnus,
> To meet Mark Antony. *(lines 227–8)*

A guardsman announces 'a rural fellow' who has come to bring her figs. Cleopatra knows he is the countryman who brings her the means of her death. She reflects on how such a lowly agent can bring her freedom, and declares herself utterly firm in her resolve, unlike the ever-changing moon:

> What poor an instrument
> May do a noble deed! He brings me liberty.

My resolution's placed, and I have nothing
Of woman in me. Now from head to foot
I am marble-constant; now the fleeting moon
No planet is of mine.   *(lines 235–40)*

The comic episode in which the Clown (the 'rural fellow') delivers
the basket that contains the deadly snakes is rich in ironic allusions to
death and sex. Many productions have highlighted the sinister aspects
of the Clown's role as death-bringer; others have played up the comic
effects. Like the gravediggers' appearance in *Hamlet*, this episode is
typically Shakespearian with its intrusion of comedy into tragedy (see
page 69). The Clown's curiously expressed warnings, his tales of
those who died from the snake's bite, his talk of immortality and of a
woman being 'a dish for the gods', lead up to his departing
valediction: 'I wish you joy o'th'worm.' The scene is set for Cleopatra's
bid for immortality in a magnificently staged death:

Give me my robe. Put on my crown. I have
Immortal longings in me.   *(lines 274–5)*

As her women dress her, Cleopatra imagines Antony calling to her,
praising the 'noble act' she is about to perform. She hears him
mocking Caesar's luck, and cries out that she comes to join him,
calling him 'Husband' for the first time in the play. She imagines
herself purged of all grossness, and beyond the earthly world. Only the
higher elements of fire and air are suitable to that exalted world of love
after death to which she aspires:

I am fire and air; my other elements
I give to baser life.   *(lines 283–4)*

Now, fully dressed in all her splendour as queen, she kisses her
women, and Iras falls dead. Shakespeare does not provide a reason for
her death. Some productions have shown Iras, a little earlier, taking a
snake from the basket and being bitten by it. A more dramatically
convincing explanation is that Iras dies of grief, so that her death
parallels that of Enobarbus. Cleopatra comments lovingly on the
gentle nature of her serving-woman's death: 'The stroke of death is as
a lover's pinch, / Which hurts, and is desired.'

Cleopatra, fearing that Iras may meet Antony first in the afterlife, takes an asp from the basket and presses it to her breast. She bids it end her life, untying the knot between body and soul, earthly limitations and infinite desire, and wishes it could jibe at Caesar, whose 'policy' she now foils:

> Come, thou mortal wretch,
> With thy sharp teeth this knot intrinsicate
> Of life at once untie. Poor venomous fool,
> Be angry, and dispatch. O, couldst thou speak,
> That I might hear thee call great Caesar ass
> Unpolicied! *(lines 297–302)*

To Charmian's 'O eastern star!', Cleopatra responds, 'Peace, peace!' and in a revealing image fantasises that the asp is her baby:

> Dost thou not see my baby at my breast,
> That sucks the nurse asleep? *(lines 303–4)*

Imagining her death to be 'As sweet as balm, as soft as air, as gentle', Cleopatra calls out again to Antony, presses another asp to her, then dies. Charmian speaks a moving eulogy:

> Now boast thee, Death, in thy possession lies
> A lass unparalleled. Downy windows, close;
> And golden Phoebus never be beheld
> Of eyes again so royal! Your crown's awry;
> I'll mend it, and then play – *(lines 309–13)*

The guards clatter in, and Charmian elatedly exclaims that Caesar has sent 'Too slow a messenger'. Determined to follow her mistress, she takes a snake from the basket and encourages it to bite her. Charmian's farewell joyously celebrates Cleopatra:

> It is well done, and fitting for a princess
> Descended of so many royal kings.
> Ah, soldier! *(lines 320–2)*

Charmian's final 'Ah, soldier!' is a fine example of Shakespeare's mastery of dramatic effect. It adds depth to her character and deepens dramatic impact in a way particularly suited to *Antony and Cleopatra* as it implies a sense of longing, and the infinite possibilities that are paradoxically both denied and realised in the heroic manner of Cleopatra's death. Early in his career, Shakespeare gave dying characters long speeches reflecting on their life and death, but here, in only two words, he enables Charmian to hint at what she might have told if only she could have lived longer.

The play moves swiftly to its conclusion with the entrance first of Dolabella, then Caesar and his troops. Caesar pays tribute to Cleopatra's bravery and acknowledges that she took her life because she guessed accurately the humiliation he had intended for her ('She levelled at our purposes'). He comments on her peaceful appearance, looking as if she slept, ready to catch Antony in her powerful snare of beauty ('strong toil of grace'). His words aptly describe the lovers' relationship, for the play has shown how Antony was fatally trapped in the 'toil' of Cleopatra's enchantment. Caesar orders Cleopatra to be buried in great ceremony beside her Antony. His praise of the lovers and their turbulent lives combines sorrow for their tragic ends with acknowledgement of his own glory in bringing about their defeat:

> No grave upon the earth shall clip in it
> A pair so famous. High events as these
> Strike those that make them; and their story is
> No less in pity than his glory which
> Brought them to be lamented. *(lines 353–7)*

Act 5: Critical review

Act 5 begins with Caesar's generous salute to Antony. It seems a remarkably unstinting tribute from the man who has derided him throughout the play, regarding him with suspicion or downright hostility. Thereafter the focus of the act is unremittingly on Cleopatra, and her 'infinite variety' is again apparent as she achieves a tragic dignity in her death, yet also displays her capacity for self-delusion, duplicity and pettiness.

Her rage at Seleucus, who reveals that she is attempting to deceive Caesar, is deeply ironic. She has in fact lied about the true extent of her wealth. It is a sign of her self-centredness that she condemns the man who tells the truth.

Cleopatra knows that Caesar's promises are false. It is his intention to display her in triumph in Rome that finally resolves her for death. The notion that 'Some squeaking Cleopatra' will 'boy' her greatness is abhorrent to her. Shakespeare here deliberately draws attention to the stage practice of his own time: his Cleopatra was indeed played by a boy. Such self-conscious acknowledgement of the actor's gender is today called meta-theatre (theatre about theatre), and adds depth to the play, though the irony is largely lost to modern audiences (except in the occasional all-male production, as at London's Globe Theatre in 1998).

The episode of the Clown who brings the asp illustrates another of Shakespeare's dramatic techniques. Just as in *Hamlet* and *Macbeth* he had brought the gravediggers and the Porter into the tragedy, now he introduces another comic, low-status character. The episode delays, yet strangely intensifies, the tragic development and, as in the other tragedies, provides a realistic, earthy perspective on the high drama that is being played out.

But the most important dramatic feature of Act 5 is how Shakespeare ensures that Cleopatra achieves full tragic status. She tells of her dream, which creates an awesomely heroic, mythical vision of Antony. She fantasises about the eternity in which she and Antony will transcend death in immortal reunion. And she accepts death with unqualified bravery. The manner in which her death is enacted represents a triumph over Caesar, the world, and death itself.

Contexts

The hugely enjoyable film *Shakespeare in Love* portrays a popular belief about the source of Shakespeare's creativity. It shows him suffering from 'writer's block', unable to put pen to paper, with no idea of how to write his next play. But all is resolved when he meets a beautiful young girl. His love for her sparks an overwhelming flow of creative energy – and he writes *Romeo and Juliet*!

It is an attractive idea, and the film presents it delightfully, but the truth of the matter is far more complex. Like every other writer, Shakespeare was influenced by many factors other than his own personal experience. The society of his time, its practices, beliefs and language in political and economic affairs, culture and religion, were the raw materials on which his imagination worked.

This section identifies the contexts from which *Antony and Cleopatra* emerged: the wide range of different influences which fostered Shakespeare's creativity as he wrote the play. These contexts ensured that *Antony and Cleopatra* contains reminders of everyday life, and the familiar knowledge, assumptions, beliefs and values of Elizabethan and Jacobean England. In particular, the play shows how Shakespeare turned what he read into superb drama.

What did Shakespeare write?

Scholars generally agree that Shakespeare wrote *Antony and Cleopatra* some time around 1606, shortly after *King Lear* and *Macbeth*. What was the play that Shakespeare wrote and his audiences heard? No one knows for certain because his original script has not survived, nor have any handwritten amendments he might subsequently have made. So what is the origin of the text of the play you are studying? *Antony and Cleopatra* was first published in 1623 (seven years after Shakespeare's death) in the volume known as the First Folio, which contains 36 of his plays. In the Folio, the play has no act or scene divisions, and is titled as both *The Tragedie of Anthonie, and Cleopatra* and as *Anthony and Cleopater*.

Today, all editions of *Antony and Cleopatra* are based on the First Folio version. But the edition of the play you are using will vary in many minor respects from other editions. That is because although every editor of the play uses the Folio version, each one makes a multitude of different judgements about such matters as spelling, punctuation, stage directions (entrances and exits, asides, etc.), scene locations and other features. You may even find that the number of scenes varies (usually in Act 4), although most editions contain either 42 or 43 scenes.

So the text of *Antony and Cleopatra* is not as stable as you might think. This is no reason for dismay, but rather an opportunity to think about how the differences reflect what actually happens in performance. Every new production cuts, adapts and amends the text to present its own unique version of *Antony and Cleopatra*. This Guide follows the New Cambridge edition of the play (also used in the Cambridge School Shakespeare edition).

What did Shakespeare read?

Shakespeare's genius lay in his ability to transform what he read into gripping drama. This section is therefore about the influence of genre: the literary context of *Antony and Cleopatra* (what critics today call 'intertextuality': the way texts influence each other). And there is one single text that very obviously influenced Shakespeare as he wrote *Antony and Cleopatra*. He found the story of Antony and Cleopatra (and stories for his other Roman plays, *Julius Caesar* and *Coriolanus*) in *The Lives of the Noble Grecians and Romans*. Written by the Greek biographer Plutarch (approx. AD 46–120), it was translated into English by Sir Thomas North, and first published in 1579. In Shakespeare's time, North's translation of Plutarch was very popular among educated people, who believed they could learn valuable lessons about vice and virtue from studying the lives of famous men.

Plutarch wrote biographies of such men, telling anecdotes about their lives to illustrate a moral or historical lesson. His 'Life of Marcus Antonius' is the longest biography in the *Lives*, and Plutarch sees Antony as a hero brought low by tragic infatuation, a great general 'made so subject to a woman's will'. Plutarch is censorious of Cleopatra, blaming her for Antony's loss of virtue: 'if any spark of goodness or hope of rising were left him, Cleopatra quenched it straight and made it worse than before'. Shakespeare's dramatic imagination was fired by what he read, and he follows Plutarch's account of Antony's life very closely. Almost every scene in the play is based on a passage or passages from Plutarch.

Shakespeare revised and selected from what he read when shaping his writing in order to increase its dramatic effect. He omits or compresses some historical events (Antony's campaigns in Parthia occupy about 20 per cent of Plutarch's biography, but Shakespeare mentions these in passing in the brief scene with Ventidius that opens Act 3). He invents other events, and frequently puts Plutarch's own critical attitudes into the mouth of Roman characters. Shakespeare makes both Antony and Cleopatra much more complex dramatic characters than they appear in the *Lives*. The audience is able to see them from many different perspectives, through the eyes of other characters. Shakespeare also gives their love and their death a nobility not found in Plutarch's account. Shakespeare also darkens some characters, making Caesar more devious and heightening Antony's flaws. For example, whereas in Plutarch Antony treats Octavia kindly, is married to her for eight years and has children by her, Shakespeare's compression of the timescale makes Antony seem much crueller to Octavia and much more evidently under Cleopatra's spell.

Shakespeare also greatly expands the role of Enobarbus from the briefest of mentions in Plutarch. Enobarbus becomes a major character, a close and trusted friend of Antony. Rather like Kent and the Fool in *King Lear*, he is both loyal and sceptical, a gruff and ironic choric commentator on events. But at one point in the play, this sardonic, pragmatic character soars into lyrical verse as he describes Cleopatra's meeting with Antony upon the river of Cydnus. At this point, and others in the play, Shakespeare follows Plutarch's prose very closely, transforming it into inspired dramatic verse, as the following extracts show.

Plutarch

> She disdained to set forward otherwise but to take her barge in the river of Cydnus, the poop whereof was of gold, the sails of purple, and the oars of silver, which kept stroke in rowing after the sound of the music of flutes, hautboys, citterns, viols, and such other instruments as they played upon in the barge. And now for the person of herself: she was laid under a pavilion of cloth of gold of tissue, apparelled and attired like the goddess Venus commonly drawn in picture, and hard by her, on either hand of her, pretty fair boys apparelled as

painters do set forth god Cupid, with little fans in their hands, with the which they fanned wind upon her.

Shakespeare

> The barge she sat in, like a burnished throne
> Burned on the water. The poop was beaten gold;
> Purple the sails, and so perfumèd that
> The winds were lovesick with them. The oars were silver,
> Which to the tune of flutes kept stroke, and made
> The water which they beat to follow faster,
> As amorous of their strokes. For her own person,
> It beggared all description: she did lie
> In her pavilion – cloth of gold, of tissue –
> O'erpicturing that Venus where we see
> The fancy outwork nature. On each side her
> Stood pretty dimpled boys, like smiling Cupids,
> With divers-coloured fans, whose wind did seem
> To glow the delicate cheeks which they did cool,
> And what they undid did.

(Act 2 Scene 2, lines 201–15)

In Shakespeare's time, such 'imitation' was a universally acclaimed practice. All playwrights (and school pupils) were encouraged to 'imitate', and were applauded for their ability to transform someone else's language into their own version.

Although the 'imitation' is clear, so too are the strikingly imaginative changes and subtle additions. For example, Plutarch's 'pretty fair boys apparelled as painters do set forth god Cupid' is transformed into the vividly concise 'pretty dimpled boys, like smiling Cupids', and the ambiguous, antithetical effect of their fans on Cleopatra is added: 'To glow the delicate cheeks which they did cool, / And what they undid did'.

Perhaps Shakespeare's most masterly dramatic stroke is to have Enobarbus deliver the speech. The blunt, cynical soldier here speaks lyrically and admiringly, quite contrary to his usual style, and this makes his extraordinarily sensual portrayal of Cleopatra appear even more believable and real. And by placing the speech almost immediately after Antony has agreed to a politically convenient arranged marriage to Octavia, Shakespeare infuses it with dramatic irony: the audience knows Antony will be unable to resist Cleopatra's allure.

What was Shakespeare's England like?

A Jacobean audience watching *Antony and Cleopatra* would have recognised many aspects of their own time and place. All kinds of fleeting allusions in the play which today need explanation would have been easily understood. When Antony claims that once kings would flock instantly to him 'Like boys unto a muss' (Act 3 Scene 13, line 93), Shakespeare's audience would have recognised the image of a game in which children scrambled eagerly for things thrown on the ground. Similarly, when Antony speaks contemptuously of flatterers who 'spanieled me at heels' and now 'discandy, melt their sweets / On blossoming Caesar' (Act 4 Scene 12, lines 20–3), they would have been reminded both of the fawning affection of spaniel dogs and the Jacobean custom of feeding dogs with sweetmeats during meals.

As most Jacobeans attended church regularly, the implications of biblical references in the play would have been quickly appreciated. When Antony is raging against Cleopatra's sexual infidelity, he vehemently wishes that he was 'Upon the hill of Basan, to outroar / The hornèd herd!' Antony's cry would have struck home to audiences in two ways. They would recognise the reference to the horns of a cuckold (a deceived husband), and they would also hear the anguished words of the Old Testament psalmist who fears that God has deserted him (Psalm 22 begins 'My God, my God, why hast thou forsaken me?' and includes being mocked by 'strong bulls of Basan'). A number of critics have claimed that Jacobeans would recall Christ's Last Supper in Antony's farewell to his servants (Act 4 Scene 2, lines 11–34), and would hear in Antony's death scene echoes of the Bible's vision of the end of the world. For example, Cleopatra's 'O sun, / Burn the great sphere thou mov'st in' and 'The crown o'th'earth doth melt' (Act 4 Scene 15, lines 10–11 and 65) recall the Book of Revelation's image of the world shaking and cracking. The same book has been suggested as the source of the imagery in Cleopatra's dream of Antony (Act 5 Scene 2, lines 78–91).

Similarly, Jacobean audiences had a greater knowledge of mythology than is common today. Classical figures like Mars and Venus would have been more readily perceived as mythical counterparts of Antony and Cleopatra (Mars, god of war, was defeated by Venus, goddess of love). Indeed John Danby confidently asserts:

> In *Antony and Cleopatra* he [Shakespeare] is making his own adjustments to the new Jacobean tastes. The play is Shakespeare's study of Mars and Venus . . . painted for us again and again on the canvases of his time.

So, too, the story of the legendary hero Hercules, subjugated by Omphale, the Amazon queen, would have been familiar from the account in Ovid's *Metamorphoses*, which was compulsory reading for all grammar school students. Omphale switched clothes with Hercules, setting him to the female task of spinning while she posed with his club. For most Jacobeans, the play's frequent allusions to Hercules needed little or no explanation: he resembles Antony in being both a mighty conqueror and an all-powerful hero in thrall to a queen who humiliates him. You can discover on page 54 why Jacobeans would have heard echoes of the story of Hercules and the shirt of Nessus when Antony rages at Cleopatra's betrayal of him.

Another pair of lovers in classical mythology are referred to in the play as models for Antony and Cleopatra: Dido and Aeneas. Again, many Jacobeans would have known the story (either from Ovid's *Heroides* or from Virgil's *Aeneid*) and would have understood its relevance to the play's lovers. Aeneas was a Trojan hero who, returning from the siege of Troy, was tempted by Dido, queen of Carthage. But he abandoned his passionate relationship with her, leaving Carthage to become the legendary founder of Rome. His desertion caused Dido to kill herself from grief.

The Commentary section contains other references to the knowledge and customs of Jacobean times (see, for example, pages 9, 25, 50 and 60). What follows is a brief discussion of particular features of Shakespeare's England that critics have claimed are important for understanding the play: Queen Elizabeth, King James, King Christian IV, beliefs about Rome and Egypt, and changing conceptions of honour.

Queen Elizabeth I

Victor Kiernan, speaking of the play's resonances for Shakespeare's contemporaries, has asserted that 'Cleopatra must have reminded many of Mary Queen of Scots, a more than half-foreign woman, fond of billiards and of wandering the streets, and England's enemy as Cleopatra was Rome's'. Other critics have seen in the play similarities between Cleopatra and Queen Elizabeth I. They have argued that a Jacobean audience, hearing Cleopatra's boast that she will 'Appear there for a man' at the battle of Actium, would have been reminded of Elizabeth's masculine language when she defiantly faced the challenge of the Spanish Armada. They have found in Cleopatra's magnificent display in her barge on the river of Cydnus echoes of the royal pageants staged for Elizabeth, which sometimes included sea spectacles.

But a more convincing connection with Queen Elizabeth lies in the fact that the subject matter of *Antony and Cleopatra* was politically dangerous in the first decade of the seventeenth century. It was the story of a great hero betrayed by a queen, and some of Shakespeare's contemporaries saw a disturbing comparison with Elizabeth and her one-time favourite, the Earl of Essex. In the closing years of Elizabeth's reign, Fulke Greville had written a play about Antony and Cleopatra, but had burned his manuscript after the failure of the rebellion of the Earl of Essex in 1601. All too aware of the wrath of an aged queen, Greville feared his play would be 'construed or strained to a personating of vices in the present government'. Greville clearly appreciated that such a play raised dangerous questions about lust, power and imperial aspiration.

Shakespeare's acting company had been marginally involved in the Essex plot. They had been paid to perform *Richard II* (showing the deposition of a monarch) the day before the revolt. The players escaped punishment, but it seems possible that the episode made Shakespeare alter his playwriting plans. He had written *Julius Caesar* in 1599 and probably intended to follow it with a play about the break-up of the Triumvirate (Octavius Caesar, Antony and Lepidus). But he delayed writing *Antony and Cleopatra* until 1606 because he recognised that to perform it during Elizabeth's reign could have been interpreted as critical comment on the politics of the time.

King James I

Even in 1606, however, the subject matter of *Antony and Cleopatra* was potentially hazardous for a playwright to explore. James was a king who insisted on his divine right to govern, and was noted for his anger at any challenge he saw to his God-given power. As Margot Heinemann argues, it was a matter

> of subversive ideas latent in the popularising of classical history, questioning the authority of absolute monarchy and the legitimacy of dictatorial rule

Many Jacobeans interpreted the political shift in Rome from republican power to the imperial rule of one man (Octavius Caesar) as corrupt and dangerous. They feared a similar process might be at work under King James as he sought increasingly to limit the power of Parliament and extend his own. From the point of view of James and his supporters, the notion of a republic was an anathema, and they distrusted Plutarch, who they felt was biased against monarchy. *Antony and Cleopatra* might end in the triumph of Caesar and the prospect of a 'time of universal peace', but that triumph and peace were put into question by the many different viewpoints expressed in Shakespeare's drama.

Nonetheless, Caesar's line 'The time of universal peace is near' (Act 4 Scene 6, line 5) is taken by some scholars to be an acknowledgement of King James I, England's own 'modern Augustus', whose policy was also a new order of peace. H Neville Davies, for example, has no doubts as to the correspondence between James and Caesar:

> . . . it is inconceivable that a dramatist late in 1606, the time when Shakespeare is usually supposed to have been writing or planning his play, could have failed to associate Caesar Augustus and the ruler (King James) whose propaganda was making just that connection.

That 'propaganda' included James' coronation medal, which depicted him wearing a laurel wreath and had a Latin inscription describing him as 'Caesar Augustus of Britain'. A host of celebratory verses were also written to James as 'England's Caesar'; and for his ceremonial entry to London, triumphal arches and a statue of Peace were created, and welcoming speeches hailed him as a successor to Augustus. Ben Jonson wrote an ode for the pageant, wishing 'lasting glory to AUGUSTUS state', and later books and sermons made parallels between James and Caesar Augustus. James' motto *beati pacifici* ('Blessed are the peace makers' from Jesus' Sermon on the Mount) expressed his domestic and foreign policy, both dedicated to peace. It is also significant that Jesus' birth was in the reign of Caesar Augustus.

Davies provides a host of other contemporary examples that link James with Augustus (Caesar in the play). James' determination to unite the three realms of England, Scotland and Wales into a unified Britain finds its parallel in *Antony and Cleopatra*, 'a play that shows the transition from triumvirate to Augustan empire'. Whilst some critics have argued that the play's jaundiced view of politics is an implicit critique of such centralisation of power, Davies argues that Shakespeare saw the merits of the unification of Britain, but 'adopted a highly ambiguous attitude towards the policies and person of his unattractive sovereign'. That ambiguity is revealed in the character of Octavius Caesar, who has been variously viewed as a Machiavellian opportunist, self-interested, cold and ambitious, and as 'noble, well-intentioned and generally just . . . a model of political wisdom'. Once again, Davies confidently detects how Shakespeare had James in mind as he wrote *Antony and Cleopatra*:

> Inevitably, the clever, scheming, canny, cautious Scotsman (James), the new Augustus whose theoretically admirable peace policy seemed in actuality less golden than the vigorous turmoil it replaced, provided Shakespeare with a sufficiently parallel life to supplement what he read in North [North's translation of Plutarch, see pages 71–3].

King Christian IV

The four-week visit to England in 1606 of King James' brother-in-law, Christian IV of Denmark, is also argued by some scholars to have provided Shakespeare with a living model for Antony. Christian was a vigorous, larger than life figure, eleven years older than James. His reputation was that of a passionately active military man, able to endure the hardships of campaigning. Christian's voyage to the Arctic had acquired legendary status with tales of feasts, orgies, entertainments and even (recalling the Thidias episode in the play) whippings of captured sea captains. Similar exotic claims were made about Christian's extravagant behaviour at his own coronation, his prowess in martial competitions, and his sexual appetite. He was also famed for his drinking: he was rumoured to down 30 to 40 goblets of wine in an evening and to be often carried to bed paralytically drunk. In all such matters, he was the living antithesis of King James.

Davies makes much of 'two extraordinary shipboard feasts' for Christian given on ships moored on the Thames, and suggests these provided a real-life source for the drinking scene on Pompey's galley in *Antony and Cleopatra* (Act 2 Scene 7). He claims that Shakespeare probably participated in some of the many lavish entertainments laid on for Christian's visit to King James (from one of which, Christian was carried out, drunk), and speculates:

> If Shakespeare looked for a modern Antony to compare with the neo-Augustus (James), he could have found no better likeness than the king of Denmark.

Rome and Egypt

Shakespeare's contemporaries were fascinated by Roman history, and they often compared London with Rome. London dominated England, just as Rome had come to dominate Italy. The Elizabethans and Jacobeans felt they could learn moral and political lessons from Rome's ideals, families, institutions and characters. It provided a model to guide both individual conduct and public affairs. In a sense, many educated Jacobeans regarded themselves as the heirs of Rome. As suggested above, in Tudor and Stuart times the empire that emerged under Caesar Augustus was seen as a valuable exemplar for unity and peace after the divisions of the Wars of the Roses in the fifteenth century.

But if Rome epitomised the ideals that Jacobeans held in high regard, the popular stereotype of Egypt represented their opposite. Shakespeare wrote the play at a time when European colonial expansion in the Americas was rapidly gathering pace. European Christians typically believed in their ethnic superiority over the native races of the New World, who were seen as heathen, savage and treacherous by nature, repaying kindness with deceit. Even the colour of their skin was held to be a mark of their less-than-human status. As trade and conquest spread eastward, similar prejudices characterised European perceptions of the peoples of Egypt and beyond. Travellers' tales, the reports of sailors and merchants, reinforced the received idea that had come down through classical literature (for example from Plutarch) that 'the Orient' was a strange and mysterious place, exotic and deeply suspect. Its inhabitants were regarded as idle and luxury-loving, unreliable and devious. Prejudice was compounded by ignorance; for example, most Jacobeans believed that gypsies were really Egyptians.

Shakespeare thus inherited a tradition that Rome represented the virtues of nobleness, discipline and restraint, and that the East was a dangerously seductive place for the self-controlled, hard-working European. Those beliefs had shaped Plutarch's account of Antony, and they flourished just as strongly 1500 years later in the England of Shakespeare's time. Jacobeans watching the play would have found their prejudices towards 'the East' confirmed. Those warped perceptions were further compounded by the sexual stereotyping of women as naturally devious. Misogyny and racism constructed Cleopatra as the archetypal barbarian, a 'stranger': a dangerous creature whose passion and practice of excess would corrupt Europeans.

Changing ideas of honour

Several critics, notably Jonathan Dollimore, have argued that *Antony and Cleopatra* reflects changing conceptions of honour in Shakespeare's England. Whilst 'honour' was vastly important to the Jacobean aristocracy, it was no longer wholly or mainly seen in terms of bravery and success in battle. That ideal of martial potency, so prominent in medieval times, declined as warfare became increasingly professionalised and under the command of the state: military glory was to be obtained within the context of the power structure of the body politic. Dollimore sees in Antony a reflection of that Jacobean conception of honour: Antony may think of himself as omnipotent, but his past military achievement derives from the power of Rome and its armies. His challenge to Caesar to meet him in personal combat is exposed as foolish: honour comes from the command of armies, not from face-to-face engagement.

In Shakespeare's England, although military bravery was still honoured and acclaimed, it was increasingly challenged and undermined by those aristocrats who became bureaucrats and policy-makers. Men like William Cecil and Robert Cecil became much more powerful than the militarists through successful diplomacy and the masterminding of seemingly mundane tasks like organising and managing taxation of the nation-state. They outmanouevred the less politically skilled aristocrats who clung to the older ideal that a nobleman's most important service to a sovereign or a state lay on the battlefield. Antony (like Coriolanus, and the chivalry-loving Hotspur of *King Henry IV Part 1*) can be seen as Shakespeare's portrayal of an aristocrat whose ideals belonged to an earlier age and were out of place both in republican Rome and in Jacobean England.

Shakespeare's own life

This section began with the film *Shakespeare in Love*. It is a delightful fantasy which gives the impression that the inspiration for *Romeo and Juliet* was Shakespeare's own personal experience of falling in love. Today, examiners give little or no credit to approaches which interpret *Antony and Cleopatra* in the context of Shakespeare's emotional life.

Nonetheless, it is worth mentioning three 'personal' matters. First, *Antony and Cleopatra* marks a significant development in Shakespeare's playwriting career. In the preceding five years he had written (among other plays) four great tragedies: *Hamlet*, *Othello*, *King Lear* and *Macbeth*. *Antony and Cleopatra* is a very different type of tragedy. The play's expansive style, exceptionally free blank verse and imagery that leaps dazzlingly from association to association, and its remarkable number of shared lines (for an analysis of these language features, see pages 82–91), might be seen as anticipating the open-endedness of the 'romances': Shakespeare's 'last plays' (*Pericles*, *The Winter's Tale*, *Cymbeline* and *The Tempest*) that were to come in the following five years.

Second, Shakespeare had helped to introduce a new fluidity into the staging practices of the time. That he was a master of these new techniques is clearly shown in the play's large number of short scenes, which flow swiftly from place to place, almost cinematic in effect.

And third, Shakespeare's acting company must surely have contained at least one extraordinarily gifted boy actor. He had recently played Lady Macbeth, and it is at least possible that that fact might have prompted Shakespeare to turn again to Plutarch, knowing he had a young actor of outstanding talent, capable of taking on the phenomenally demanding role of Cleopatra (and the very different, but equally exacting role of Volumnia in *Coriolanus* which almost immediately followed).

Language

Ben Jonson famously remarked that Shakespeare 'wanted art' (lacked technical skill). But Jonson's comment is mistaken, as is the popular image of Shakespeare as a 'natural' writer, utterly spontaneous, inspired only by his imagination. Shakespeare possessed a profound knowledge of the language techniques of his own and previous times. In his plays he skilfully employs a range of language styles to create characters, themes and atmosphere.

Nowhere is Shakespeare's skill more evident than in *Antony and Cleopatra*. Roman speech is business-like and controlled; Egyptian speech sensuous and relaxed. He gives each character a distinctive register, turns nouns into verbs ('boy my greatness'), creates new words with prefixes ('unseminar'd', 'unhair'), and uses an extraordinary range of imagery for a multitude of purposes: Cleopatra dismisses her youthful inexperience in choosing lovers with 'My salad days, / When I was green in judgement'. The two ageing lovers indulge in imagination-stirring hyperbole: 'Eternity was in our lips and eyes', 'His legs bestrid the ocean; his reared arm / Crested the world', 'Now from head to foot / I am marble-constant'. Through such exalted language, Antony and Cleopatra create their own mythic destiny: the vision of themselves as heroic, immortal lovers.

What follows are some of the language techniques Shakespeare uses in *Antony and Cleopatra* to intensify dramatic effect, create mood and character, and so produce memorable theatre. As you read the play, always keep in mind that Shakespeare wrote for the stage, and that actors will employ a wide variety of verbal and non-verbal methods to exploit the dramatic possibilities of the language. They will use the full range of their voices and accompany the words with appropriate expressions, gestures and actions.

Imagery

The language of *Antony and Cleopatra* abounds in imagery (sometimes called 'figures' or 'figurative language'): vivid words and phrases that help create the atmosphere of the play as they conjure up emotionally charged pictures and associations in the imagination. Imagery enhances and deepens imaginative effect, and gives insight into characters' feelings and thoughts. The imagery of *Antony and Cleopatra* is extraordinarily varied, often shifting dazzlingly within a single short speech. For example, when Antony discovers that many of his followers have deserted him, he exclaims:

> The hearts
> That spanieled me at heels, to whom I gave
> Their wishes, do discandy, melt their sweets
> On blossoming Caesar; and this pine is barked
> That overtopped them all.
>
> *(Act 4 Scene 12, lines 20–4)*

The images switch rapidly as brave men ('hearts') become fawning dogs ('spanieled me at heels'), who melt away ('discandy') and pour the gifts and honours Antony had awarded them ('melt their sweets') on Caesar whose fortunes prosper like a flowering tree ('blossoming'). Antony imagines himself in contrast to be like a dying pine tree, stripped of its bark, when once he towered over all men ('overtopped'). In comparing his former followers to dogs, Antony expresses his disgust at their behaviour: they have run from one leader to another, and there is even a possible association in the complex imagery of dogs urinating against trees, lending a sarcastic note to the phrase 'melt their sweets'.

Shakespeare's imagery makes use of metaphor, simile and personification. All are comparisons which in effect substitute one thing (the image) for another (the thing described).

- A *simile* compares one thing to another using 'like' or 'as'. Scarus contemptuously describes how Cleopatra fled from the battle of Actium 'like a cow in June', and how Antony followed her 'like a doting mallard'. Cleopatra, seeing Iras fall and die, declares, 'The stroke of death is as a lover's pinch', and feels her own death 'As sweet as balm, as soft as air, as gentle –', but does not complete the final simile.
- A *metaphor* is also a comparison, suggesting that two dissimilar things are actually the same. For Cleopatra music is the 'moody food / Of us that trade in love', and she thinks of suicide as that thing 'Which shackles accidents and bolts up change': imprisons chance and the transformations of time.

- *Personification* turns all kinds of things into persons, giving them human feelings or attributes. Death and Fortune figure prominently in the play. Defeated at Actium, Antony is defiant: 'Fortune knows / We scorn her most when most she offers blows.' He later brags, 'The next time I do fight / I'll make Death love me'. But after his final defeat by Caesar, and feeling betrayed by Cleopatra, he exclaims, 'Fortune and Antony part here; even here / Do we shake hands.' After Cleopatra dies, Charmian cries out, 'Now boast thee, Death, in thy possession lies / A lass unparalleled.'

Early critics such as John Dryden and Doctor Johnson were critical of Shakespeare's fondness for imagery. They felt that many images obscured meaning and detracted attention from the subjects they represented. Over the past 200 years, however, critics, poets and audiences have increasingly valued Shakespeare's imagery. They recognise how he uses it to provoke thought and to give pleasure as it stirs the audience's imagination, deepens the dramatic impact of particular moments or moods, creates character, and intensifies meaning and emotional force. Images carry powerful significance far deeper than their surface meanings. The following are some of the clusters of repeated images which echo and reflect the play's many oppositions and paradoxes, and help create a sense of its themes.

Melting

Antony's decline is reflected in the many images of melting, fading, dissolving and losing form. The image-cluster begins very early in the first scene as Antony refuses to hear Caesar's messengers: 'Let Rome in Tiber melt'. Cleopatra, enraged by Antony's marriage to Octavia, cries, 'Melt Egypt into Nile'. Antony, angry that his servants are slow to respond, exclaims, 'Authority melts from me'; and at his death Cleopatra laments, 'The crown o'th'earth doth melt'. Charmian, seeing Cleopatra close to death, cries out:

> Dissolve, thick cloud, and rain, that I may say
> The gods themselves do weep!   *(Act 5 Scene 2, lines 293–4)*

Shakespeare invents words to suggest the process of dissolution: 'disponge', 'discandy', 'dislimn'. All have the sense of liquefying, deliquescence, losing shape. Enobarbus calls for 'The poisonous damp of night' to 'disponge' upon him to take his life. Antony's followers 'discandy' (melt) as they desert him; Cleopatra, longing to regain Antony's affection, appeals to a storm to drop 'discandying' poisoned hailstones on her to 'Dissolve' her life should she be cold-hearted towards Antony. Near his end, Antony, utterly defeated and believing himself betrayed by Cleopatra, imagines his identity dissolving like the changing shape of clouds:

> That which is now a horse, even with a thought
> The rack dislimns and makes it indistinct
> As water is in water.   (*Act 4 Scene 14, lines 9–11*)

Feeding and hunger

Many images of food and eating are associated with Cleopatra. She herself speaks of music as the 'moody food / Of us that trade in love'. Enobarbus is certain that Antony will never be able to break free of her because 'Other women cloy / The appetites they feed, but she makes hungry / Where most she satisfies.' Elsewhere she is described as an 'Egyptian dish', and 'A morsel for a monarch'. But Antony angrily taunts her in demeaning food imagery: 'I found you as a morsel cold upon / Dead Caesar's trencher; nay, you were a fragment [leftover] / Of Cneius Pompey's'.

A major function of such imagery is to reinforce the impression of Egypt as a place of luxurious excess where prodigious banquets are all part of the hedonistic, luxury-loving life so different from the restraint of Rome, where Caesar regards it all as 'lascivious wassails'. But the food imagery has more sinister implications, for example as Enobarbus imagines the coming wars between Antony and Caesar to be like the world eating itself ('pair of chaps' = jaws):

> Then, world, thou hast a pair of chaps, no more;
> And throw between them all the food thou hast,
> They'll grind the one the other.   (*Act 3 Scene 5, lines 11–13*)

The world

The word 'world' becomes a recurrent metaphor in the play, reinforcing the sense of grandeur and the huge scope of the drama. In the very first scene, Antony is described as 'The triple pillar of the world', and other such world-dominating images of him recur: 'the greatest soldier of the world', 'The demi-Atlas of this earth', 'the worship of the whole world', 'the greatest prince o'th'world', 'The crown o'th'earth'. Cleopatra speaks of her dream of Antony whose 'reared arm / Crested the world'. Other characters are similarly pictured in world terms. Pompey is spoken of as endangering 'The sides o'th'world'. As a servant carries out the drunken Lepidus, Enobarbus jokes that he 'bears / The third part of the world'. Antony calls Cleopatra 'O thou day o'th'world'; and she mockingly calls Caesar 'Sole sir o'th'world'.

Other vivid images also evoke the worldwide range of the play. Caesar complains that Antony is 'levying / The kings o'th'earth for war', and later speaks of the universal peace that his victory will bring to 'the three-nooked world'. Cleopatra greets Antony, who has come unhurt from a victory over Caesar, with 'com'st thou smiling from / The world's great snare uncaught?' In quite a different mood some scenes later, as she looks down from her monument and sees the wounded Antony, she produces a hyperbolically apocalyptic image of world destruction:

> O sun,
> Burn the great sphere thou mov'st in; darkling stand
> The varying shore o'th'world!
>
> *(Act 4 Scene 15, lines 10–12)*

Imagery of vacillation

Cleopatra's image just noted speaks of 'The varying shore o'th'world'. That notion of fluctuation or inconstancy runs through *Antony and Cleopatra*, reflecting the ever-changing moods of the two major characters, and the uncertainty that characterises so much of the play. For example, Caesar sees the common people as inherently unreliable, changing allegiance from leader to leader:

> Like to a vagabond flag upon the stream,
> Goes to and back, lackeying the varying tide
> To rot itself with motion.   *(Act 1 Scene 4, lines 44–6)*

In a similar image based on the movement of water, Antony describes Octavia's hesitation when she finds herself caught between affection for her brother and himself. She 'stands upon the swell at the full of tide' and will therefore have to be carried one way or the other:

> the swansdown feather,
> That stands upon the swell at the full of tide,
> And neither way inclines   *(Act 3 Scene 2, lines 48–50)*

Cosmic and transcendental images

Antony and Cleopatra frequently use cosmic images, often to describe each other. The sun, moon, stars and heavens echo through the play. Antony, thinking Cleopatra is unfaithful to him, rages that his 'good stars' are in 'th'abysm of hell'. He sees his downfall predicted in her betrayal: 'our terrene moon is now eclipsed, / And it portends alone the fall of Antony'. One of the guards who discover the wounded Antony cries out, 'The star is fall'n.' Cleopatra, at her first sight of the wounded Antony, cries out to the sun to burn 'the great sphere' it moves in: the death of one man calls for the death of the universe. As she draws him up, she wishes to set him 'by Jove's side', but after he dies she threatens to throw her sceptre 'at the injurious gods' in their heavens for stealing Antony, the world's 'jewel'. Later, she tells Dolabella of her dream, which again elevates Antony above common humanity:

> His face was as the heav'ns, and therein stuck
> A sun and moon, which kept their course and lighted
> This little O, the earth.   *(Act 5 Scene 2, lines 78–80)*

Antithesis

Antithesis is the opposition of words or phrases against each other, as when Iras declares, 'The bright day is done, / And we are for the dark', or when Cleopatra falsely claims, 'Mine honour was not yielded, / But conquered merely.' This setting of word against word ('bright' opposes 'dark', 'yielded' is set against 'conquered') is one of Shakespeare's favourite language devices. He uses it extensively in all his plays. Why? Because antithesis powerfully expresses conflict through its use of opposites, and conflict is the essence of all drama. In *Antony and Cleopatra*, conflict occurs in many forms: Rome against Egypt, Antony against Caesar, the lovers against each other as their emotions swing wildly. Antony's heroic past is overshadowed by his tarnished present; loyalty is contrasted with treachery. The gap between rhetoric and reality is often apparent, and there is great contrast in the way characters are described: Cleopatra, for example, is described as both 'enchanting queen' and 'triple-turned whore'. The antitheses that recur inexorably throughout the play are Shakespeare's linguistic embodiment of those conflicts.

At the very start of the play, Philo's speech contains many antitheses as he complains of Antony's decline, most notably ending with how 'The triple pillar of the world' is now 'a strumpet's fool'. Lepidus seeks to reconcile Antony and Caesar with 'Touch you the sourest points with sweetest terms'. Octavia, fearing war between Caesar and Antony, despairs 'Husband win, win brother, / Prays and destroys the prayer'. Cleopatra denies Antony's grandiose declarations of love with 'Excellent falsehood!' and later uses antithesis to irritate him:

> If you find him sad,
> Say I am dancing; if in mirth, report
> That I am sudden sick. *(Act 1 Scene 3, lines 3–5)*

Later in the same scene, Antony bids farewell to Cleopatra with a series of antitheses:

> Let us go. Come;
> Our separation so abides and flies
> That thou, residing here, goes yet with me,
> And I, hence fleeting, here remain with thee.
> *(Act 1 Scene 3, lines 102–5)*

Repetition

Different forms of language repetition contribute to the play's atmosphere, creation of character, and dramatic impact. Certain words flow like undercurrents through the dramatic narrative: 'world', 'Rome', 'honour', 'fortune'. Each impresses on the audience's mind a major theme of the play, as do the recurring images detailed on pages 84–7. 'World' establishes the huge scope and setting of the play. 'Rome' conveys the sense of immense imperial power. 'Honour' expresses the nobility which Antony and Caesar claim, but which is ironically undercut by their actions. And 'fortune' emphasises the luck that Caesar has, and Antony does not, as the wheel of fortune swings Antony from its topmost point to its lowest: 'Fortune and Antony part here', he declares after he loses the final battle.

Particular speeches contain both obvious and subtle repetitions. The final ten lines of Act 4 unite Cleopatra, Iras and Charmian in a sisterhood of death with its five repetitions of 'women' and other forms which express the female bonding that operates so strongly in the episode: 'My noble girls!', 'Our', 'Good sirs' (sometimes used to address women in Shakespeare's time), 'We'll', 'Let's' (let us), 'us', 'we' (see also page 115). The Clown who brings Cleopatra the serpents that will kill her repeatedly expresses a quite different view of women. And in Cleopatra's final moments, the agonised feeling in Charmian's 'O, break! O, break!' is contrasted with Cleopatra's calm 'Peace, peace!' and the tranquillity of 'As sweet', 'as soft', 'as gentle' as she welcomes death.

The verse of *Antony and Cleopatra* also heightens theatrical effect and deepens emotional and imaginative significance through repetitive rhythms. Enobarbus' description of Cleopatra at Cydnus has the delicate cadence and movement of the very finest poetry, unobtrusively patterned and measured (see pages 22–3). A number of scenes end in rhyming couplets: elsewhere, lines occasionally mirror each other, as when Cleopatra struggles to find suitable words to say farewell to Antony:

> Sir, you and I must part, but that's not it;
> Sir, you and I have loved, but there's not it
>
> *(Act 1 Scene 3, lines 88–9)*

Such linguistic repetitions mirror Shakespeare's dramatic construction: the continual setting of character against character, Rome against Egypt; the way that scenes reflect each other, and other repetitions, like the frequent entrance of messengers. Cleopatra's harsh treatment of the messenger who beings her news of Antony's marriage is more cruelly repeated as Antony has Thidias, Caesar's messenger, whipped for daring to kiss Cleopatra's hand. Cleopatra's fleet twice betrays Antony, and his followers increasingly desert him, as does his god, Hercules, in the eerie Scene 3 of Act 4.

Lists

One of Shakespeare's favourite language methods is to accumulate words or phrases rather like a list. His skill in knowing how to use lists dramatically is evident in the many examples in *Antony and Cleopatra*. He intensifies and varies descriptions, atmospheres and arguments as he 'piles up' item on item, incident on incident. Lists of place names and people dazzle and impress, giving a sense of the worldwide scope of the play's setting:

> He hath assembled
> Bocchus, the King of Libya; Archelaus,
> Of Cappadocia; Philadelphos, King
> Of Paphlagonia; the Thracian king, Adallas;
> King Manchus of Arabia; King of Pont;
> Herod of Jewry . . .   *(Act 3 Scene 6, lines 70–5)*

In briefer lists, Antony accurately catches Cleopatra's swiftly changing moods in 'to chide, to laugh, / To weep', and Charmian laughingly hopes for the Soothsayer to predict 'excellent fortune' for her as she catalogues her wishes:

> Let me be married to three kings in a forenoon and widow
> them all. Let me have a child at fifty, to whom Herod of Jewry
> may do homage. Find me to marry me with Octavius Caesar,
> and companion me with my mistress.
>
> *(Act 1 Scene 2, lines 25–9)*

Cleopatra threatens the messenger: 'I'll spurn thine eyes', 'I'll unhair thy head!', 'Thou shalt be whipped with wire, and stewed in brine'. More sombrely, she determines that Caesar will not triumph over her 'If knife, drugs, serpents, have / Edge, sting, or operation'. And Caesar pays tribute to Antony, listing what had once bound them together:

> my brother, my competitor
> In top of all design, my mate in empire,
> Friend and companion in the front of war,
> The arm of mine own body, and the heart
> Where mine his thoughts did kindle
>
> *(Act 5 Scene 1, lines 42–6)*

Verse and prose

How did Shakespeare decide whether to write in verse or prose? One answer is that he followed theatrical convention. Prose was traditionally used by comic and low-status characters. High-status characters spoke verse. 'Comic' scenes were written in prose, but audiences expected verse in 'serious' scenes: the poetic style was thought to be particularly suitable for moments of high dramatic or emotional intensity. Less than ten per cent of the play is in prose: the exchanges between Charmian, Iras and the Soothsayer in Act 1 Scene 2, the episode in which the Clown brings the asps to Cleopatra in Act 5 Scene 2, and some of Enobarbus' speeches in which he comments sardonically on what he sees or hears.

The verse of *Antony and Cleopatra* is mainly blank verse: unrhymed verse written in iambic pentameter. It is conventional to define iambic pentameter as a rhythm or metre in which each line has five stressed syllables (/) alternating with five unstressed syllables (×):

> × / × / × / × / × /
> If it be love indeed, tell me how much.

At school, Shakespeare had learned the technical definition of iambic pentameter. In Greek *penta* means 'five', and *iamb* means a 'foot' of two syllables: the first unstressed, the second stressed, as in 'alas' = aLAS. Shakespeare practised writing in that metre, and his early plays, such as *Titus Andronicus* or *Richard III* are very regular in rhythm (often expressed as de-DUM de-DUM de-DUM de-DUM de-DUM), and with each line 'end-stopped' (making sense on its own).

By the time he came to write *Antony and Cleopatra* (around 1606), Shakespeare used great variation in his verse. It is exceptionally free from the strict rules of convention. Very few lines are completely 'regular' (five 'beats' in order). He adds extra syllables and varies the rhythm. Many lines are not 'end-stopped', the sense running over into the following line (*enjambement*). Many lines are 'shared', as a speaker ends a speech part way through a line, which is completed by the next speaker. Some critics argue such sharing creates tension, interpersonal conflicts; others assert that it conveys a sense of genuine dialogue, with each speaker listening intently to what the other says, and replying, sometimes interrupting them.

Critical approaches

Traditional criticism

Antony and Cleopatra has always attracted less critical attention and acclaim than *Macbeth*, *King Lear*, *Othello* and *Hamlet*. One recurring feature of traditional writing about the play is how critics differ on the nature of the love of Antony and Cleopatra. Some see it as ennobling, others as reckless, destructive passion which loses them the world. Derek Traversi expresses these two traditional views as:

> . . . a tragedy of lyrical inspiration, justifying love by presenting it as triumphant over death, or . . . a remorseless exposure of human frailties, a presentation of spiritual possibilities dissipated through a senseless surrender to passion.

Another persisting aspect of traditional criticism is its condemnation of the structure of the play. The leading eighteenth-century critic Doctor Samuel Johnson (1765) asserted, 'The events . . . are produced without any art of connection or care of disposition'. In contrast, the exoticism and excess of *Antony and Cleopatra* appealed greatly to the Romantic critics of the early nineteenth century. Samuel Taylor Coleridge judged it 'the most wonderful' of all Shakespeare's plays, and described its style as 'feliciter audax', meaning 'happy valiancy' (inspired daring). William Hazlitt's enthusiasm was only just a little less tempered: 'This is a very noble play. Though not in the first class of Shakespeare's productions, it stands next to them . . . he made poetry the organ of history'.

Doctor Johnson had been critical of Shakespeare's characterisation, stating that 'no character is very strongly discriminated', but Coleridge applauded Shakespeare's profound art in creating Cleopatra: 'the sense of criminality in her passion is lessened by our insight into its depth and energy'. His view was echoed by Hazlitt, who argued that in the play, Shakespeare

> brings living men and women on the scene, who speak and act from real feelings, according to the ebbs and flows of passion

> . . . The character of Cleopatra is a masterpiece . . . voluptuous,
> ostentatious, conscious, boastful of her charms, haughty,
> tyrannical, fickle . . . she has great and unpardonable faults,
> but the grandeur of her death almost redeems them.

Later nineteenth-century writing continued the critical obsession with character. Edward Dowden's florid style is typical: 'The characters of Antony and Cleopatra insinuate themselves through the senses, trouble the blood, ensnare the imagination, invade our whole being like colour or music'. The critic with whom the expression 'character study' is most associated is A C Bradley. Around 100 years ago, Bradley delivered a course of lectures at Oxford University which were published in 1904 as *Shakespearean Tragedy*. The book is centrally concerned with *Hamlet*, *Macbeth*, *Othello* and *King Lear*, and is still in print and widely read. In the book, Bradley makes only passing references to *Antony and Cleopatra*, judging it as 'the most faultily constructed of all the tragedies', and not having 'an equal value' to the four major tragedies.

Bradley offered a sustained critical analysis of the play in a later essay: 'Shakespeare's *Antony and Cleopatra*'. He was still much concerned with character: Cleopatra is 'coquetting, tormenting, beguiling', 'an enchantress', 'her spirit is made of wind and flame'; Antony has an 'open, generous, expansive nature . . . his nature tends to splendid action and lusty enjoyment'; 'Shakespeare . . . took little interest in the character of Octavius', etc. But Bradley's discussion also ranged much wider. Like earlier critics he criticised what he saw as the play's lack of sustained narrative, its frequent scene changes and lack of action. He repeated his earlier judgement that it was 'defective in construction', and argued the play was fundamentally undramatic: 'these two and forty scenes could not possibly be acted as they stand'.

Bradley queried whether the play really was a tragedy. It was 'not painful', and had nothing purely good or evil in it. There were 'no scenes of action or passion which agitate the audience with alarm, horror, painful expectation, or absorbing sympathies and antipathies'. In the first three acts 'people converse, discuss, accuse one another, excuse themselves, mock, describe, drink together, arrange a marriage, meet and part; but they do not kill, do not even tremble or weep'. Bradley's discussion illustrates traditional critical uncertainty as to whether the lovers experience a tragic fall, and whether they succeed or are ennobled in their death. It has prompted much discussion of the play's genre: *Antony and Cleopatra* has been variously claimed to be a tragedy, a tragi-comedy, a history play, a morality play, a satire and even a 'problem play' (a play which makes the audience unsure of their moral bearings, unsure about the rights and wrongs of what they see and hear). Typically, critics who deny the play full tragic status claim there is little sense of irremediable loss, and point to the lack of tragic motivation expressed in soliloquies: neither major character is moved by guilt or terror, but, rather, acts impulsively.

Although Bradley has fallen from critical favour, his influence is still evident. Even the most modern criticism, whilst preferring to discuss characters as fictional creations in a stage drama, finds it difficult, if not impossible, to avoid writing about characters as if they were living people and making moral judgements on them. And in *Antony and Cleopatra* the two main characters have such a powerful presence that discussion of their personalities, motives and actions seems inevitable.

It would be inappropriate, however, to think of traditional criticism as solely concerned with character. The study of the play's exceptionally rich imagery has also been a major focus. W H Clemen stresses the importance of the imagery of the sea, the Nile and its creatures, and of fortune and heavenly bodies. Caroline Spurgeon finds that the images which immediately attract attention are

> images of the world, the firmament, the ocean and vastness generally . . . stimulating our imaginations to see the colossal figure of Antony, 'demi-Atlas of this earth', 'triple pillar of the world' . . .

But Spurgeon virtually ignores Cleopatra, and avoids any discussion of the sexual implications of the play's imagery. The weakness of both Spurgeon's and Clemen's studies is that both claim that the imagery gives direct access to Shakespeare's own thoughts, feelings, nature and experience. For example, Spurgeon claims that 'peep' is 'his favourite verb', and that Lepidus' plea that Antony and Caesar should discuss their differences gently shows that Shakespeare from his youth 'shrank from noisy and acrimonious argument'.

A more wide-ranging study of the play's imagery is that of Maurice

Charney. He too claims that 'world imagery' is 'the most general pattern of imagery in the play', but more extensively examines how the imagery relates to the dramatic context of the play. Charney also makes much of sword and armour imagery, which he sees as embodying the Roman concerns of war and soldiership, and of how Egypt renders Antony's sword powerless. He analyses the food imagery of the play, and identifies images of 'melting, fading, dissolving, discandying, disponging and losing of form' which convey 'the feeling of disintegration in the Roman world'.

G Wilson Knight argues for the unity of the play, finding in it 'certain symbolic images', particularly of war and love, which 'lead us from multiplicity and chaos towards unity, simplicity and coherence'. Knight's interpretation, like Bradley's, is one of transcendental optimism: the lovers achieve apotheosis and tragic dignity in death, as Antony sacrifices 'imperial magnificence' (imperial power and warrior honour) for love. Knight's grandiloquent style and urge to achieve 'closure' by imposing unity on the play have fallen out of fashion. The following quotation is typical of the cosmic style of all Knight's writing as he is carried aloft by Shakespeare's imagery and strives to unite the human and the supernatural, the concrete and the metaphysical:

> We see the protagonists, in love and war and sport, in death or life or that mystery containing both, transfigured in a transfigured universe, themselves that universe and more, outspacing the wheeling orbs of earth and heaven . . . This is the high metaphysic of love which melts life and death into a final oneness; which reality is indeed no pulseless attraction, but rather blends its single design and petalled excellence from all life and all death, all imperial splendour and sensuous delight, all strange and ethereal forms, all elements and heavenly stars; all that is natural, human, and divine, all brilliance and all glory.

In marked contrast to such purple prose, Janet Adelman's detailed examination of the play's language reveals its 'partiality of truth': the poetry with which Antony and Cleopatra construct their views of each other and the world cannot be fully trusted. John Danby similarly emphasises the unstable nature of the play. He stresses its cinematic nature, short scenes, constantly changing locations and viewpoints, and locates the tragedy not in ultimate unity, but in disjunction. For Danby, the ever-changing perspectives cannot result in the 'resolution' that tragedy is conventionally thought to achieve. Antony is caught between the irreconcilable demands of Egypt and Rome, and the play therefore has at its heart a view of the world as unstable. Danby also challenges the traditional dichotomy of the perception of Antony and Cleopatra as either besotted lovers who lose all, or as heroic lovers who triumph over death itself, redeeming themselves from the worldly defeat inflicted upon them:

> The Roman condemnation of the lovers is obviously inadequate. The sentimental reaction in their favour is equally mistaken. There is no so-called 'love-romanticism' in the play ... To go further still in sentimentality and claim that there is a 'redemption' motif in Antony and Cleopatra's love is an even more violent error ... Shakespeare may have his plays in which 'redemption' is a theme ... but *Antony and Cleopatra* is not one of them.

Modern criticism

Throughout the second half of the twentieth century and in the twenty-first, critical approaches to Shakespeare have radically challenged the style and assumptions of the traditional approaches described above. New critical approaches argue that traditional interpretations, often heavily focused on character, are individualistic and misleading. The traditional concentration on personal feelings ignores society and history, and so divorces literary, dramatic and aesthetic matters from their social context. Further, their detachment from the real world makes them elitist, sexist and apolitical.

Modern critical perspectives therefore shift the focus from individuals to how social conditions (of the world of the play and of Shakespeare's England) are reflected in characters' relationships, language and behaviour. Modern criticism also concerns itself with how social assumptions and practices at different times in history, right up to the present day, have affected interpretations of the play.

This section will explore how modern critical approaches to Shakespeare have been used to explore *Antony and Cleopatra*.

Contemporary approaches, like traditional criticism, include many different perspectives, but share common features. Modern criticism:

- is sceptical of 'character' approaches (but often uses them);
- concentrates on political, social and economic factors (arguing that these factors determine Shakespeare's creativity and audiences' and critics' interpretations);
- identifies contradictions, fragmentation and disunity in the plays;
- questions the possibility of 'happy' or 'hopeful' endings, preferring ambiguous, unsettling or sombre endings;
- produces readings that are subversive of existing social structures;
- identifies how the plays express the interests of dominant groups, particularly rich and powerful males;
- insists that 'theory' (psychological, social, etc.) is essential to produce valid readings;
- often expresses its commitment to a particular cause (for example, to feminism, or equality, or anti-colonialism, or political change);
- argues that all readings are political or ideological readings (and that traditional criticism falsely claims to be objective);
- argues that traditional approaches have always interpreted Shakespeare conservatively, in ways that confirm and maintain the interests of the elite or dominant class.

Such assumptions led John Drakakis to see *Antony and Cleopatra* as particularly open to modern theoretical approaches:

> . . . partly because of its obviously dialectical structure, but also because it traverses a range of issues that have direct relevance to current questions of history, theatre, genre, race, gender and politics.

The following discussion is therefore organised under headings which represent major contemporary critical perspectives on *Antony and Cleopatra* (political, feminist, performance, psychoanalytic, postmodern). But it is vital to appreciate that there is often overlap between the categories, and that to pigeonhole any example of criticism too precisely is to reduce its value and application. Any single critical essay may have a dominant focus, but it usually takes account of other approaches.

Political criticism

'Political criticism' is a convenient label for approaches concerned with power and social structure: in the world of the play, in Shakespeare's time and in our own. Such criticism is sceptical of traditional critics' writing about the play as a heady mixture of romantic passion and Roman history. It has no patience with the notion of the play's 'transcendent themes', as for example in the writing of Wilson Knight (see page 95), or with discussions of poetry, imagery or character that do not locate these matters in the political context of the play. Rather, it gives weight to such seemingly small incidents as Dercetus stealing Antony's sword after his botched suicide attempt. Political critics claim that such an action reveals the cynical political context of the play: a minor character like Dercetus abandons his defeated master, determined to survive and prosper in the harsh world of Roman *realpolitik* (power politics) by using the sword as his passport to Caesar's favour.

Even more emphasis is given to the short scene (Act 3 Scene 1) in which Ventidius exposes the gap between the rhetoric and the reality of the Roman state. The supreme Roman virtue, bravery and glory in war, is revealed as a sham, untruthfully claimed by leaders as a cover for their political ambitions. For example, Victor Kiernan's Marxist study of Shakespeare's plays sees Antony as 'a great man cashiered by history', caught between conflicting political systems. Kiernan argues that, as the Ventidius scene shows, both Caesar and Antony owe their stature chiefly to political self-advertisement and creation of myth. Kiernan's endeavour is to show that Shakespeare intended *Antony and Cleopatra* to be a political commentary with a clear message:

> Altogether this is a highly political, as well as romantic, drama,
> a many-sided picture of imperial Rome refracted through the
> mind of a keen observer of politics in his own day . . . It tells us
> much about Shakespeare's political philosophy, which he
> clearly wants us to comprehend. All power and greatness are
> an artificial pageant.

A well-known critic who is often called upon in support of political interpretations of Shakespeare's plays is the Polish scholar Jan Kott. Kott fought with the Polish army and underground movement against the Nazis in the Second World War (1939–45), and had direct experience of the suffering and terror caused by Stalinist repression in Poland in the years after the war. His book *Shakespeare Our Contemporary* makes parallels between the violence and cruelty of the modern world and the worlds of tyranny and despair that Shakespeare depicted in his tragedies. History, for Kott, is an oppressive force, and 'in Shakespeare history itself is the drama'.

For Kott, the ancient world reflects modern political cynicism and violence. For example, he identifies Menas' offer to cut the throats of the three triumvirs as 'one of the greatest scenes' in the play, 'a scene strikingly modern'. And for Kott, Cleopatra's decision to 'sell herself' to Caesar and so save her kingdom, shows that 'in Shakespeare's world, even rulers do not have the freedom of choice. History is not an abstract term, but a practical mechanism'. What Kott has in mind here is the notion he develops in his discussion of Shakespeare's history plays: that history is a 'Grand Mechanism', a long staircase of murder, perfidy and treachery, as ruler succeeds ruler.

Political criticism regards traditional criticism's fascination with Cleopatra's linguistic power and seductive sexuality (making hungry where most she satisfies) as racist, sexist and colonialist. Such stereotyping, political critics argue, ignores the fact that Rome's relationship with Egypt is one of conquest. Cleopatra is a victim of Roman colonisation, and an opponent of Rome's military power. Her sexuality is an integral part of the political fabric of the play, not just incidental to it. The values of Egypt as represented by Cleopatra are not simply a strange and exotic challenge to the values of Rome, but are embedded in a political struggle between the two worlds of the play. For Jonathan Dollimore, in *Antony and Cleopatra* sexual desire does not transcend politics, but is the vehicle of political and personal power:

> . . . the language of desire, far from transforming the power relations which structure this society, is wholly informed by them.

Dollimore's influential book, *Radical Tragedy*, locates Shakespeare's tragedies in the context of their times: a period of radical change. Dollimore interprets *Antony and Cleopatra* as centrally concerned with 'complex social and political relations', and with subjecting those relations to 'sceptical interrogation'. Antony operates in a world of *realpolitik*, not in a world determined by such abstract and mystifying concepts as 'Time' or 'Destiny', preferred by traditional critics. His arranged marriage with Octavia is a political affair, as is his alliance with Caesar and Lepidus against Pompey. So too is the 'policy' (Machiavellian deceit) that runs through the play (Menas' offer to murder the triumvirs, Thidias' appeal to Cleopatra to betray Antony, Cleopatra's failed attempt to conceal her wealth, etc.). Even love is described 'in terms of power; languages of possession, subjugation and conspicuous wealth'.

Dollimore therefore sees Antony as neither self-sufficient nor autonomous, but dependent on the political system in which he lives. As Enobarbus recognises, Antony's challenge to Caesar to meet him in personal single combat is simply stupid because power does not reside in individual bravery. Antony seems powerful, but his military achievement and honour rests on a power structure that has given him personal and political identity. His heroic status has been achieved through 'forces and relations of power' (Rome's military power) and it is that political structure which has conferred honour on him. In the play, as he transgresses that structure, his identity disintegrates. Thus Dollimore sees Antony, not as a hero, but as a man destroyed because he fails to comply with the values of the state which confers heroism on those who conform.

Feminist criticism

Feminism aims to achieve rights and equality for women in social, political and economic life. It challenges sexism: those beliefs and practices which result in the degradation, oppression and subordination of women. Feminist critics therefore reject 'male ownership' of criticism, in which men determined which questions were to be asked of a play and which answers were acceptable. From this standpoint, Bradley's confident assertion of Cleopatra's effect on Antony ('she destroys him') simply reveals typical Edwardian gender prejudice. Feminist critics argue that male criticism often neglects, represses or misrepresents female experience, and stereotypes or distorts women's points of view. Linda Fitz provides the clearest example of that feminist argument.

Fitz launches an all-out attack on the sexist attitudes that characterise traditional male criticism. She quotes extensively from such criticism and argues that it shows male critics 'feel personally threatened by Cleopatra' and reveals their 'deep personal fears of aggressive or manipulative women'. Her critique of the sexism that pervades the responses of male critics can be briefly summarised. It:

- creates two types of archetypical women. One condemns Cleopatra as a 'practiser of feminine wiles, mysterious, childlike, long on passion and short on intelligence – except for a sort of animal cunning'. The other praises Octavia as chaste and submissive.
- is characterised by prudery and 'distaste for the play's overt sexuality', especially for the sexual *double entendres* spoken by Cleopatra (e.g. 'O happy horse to bear the weight of Antony').
- applies double standards, finding what is praiseworthy in Antony to be damnable in Cleopatra. For example, Antony's attempt to break from Cleopatra and return to public duties in Rome is commended, but Cleopatra's attempt 'to save her political skin' in the Thidias scene (Act 3 Scene 13) is condemned.
- promotes double standards which 'seriously distort the play', stereotyping women as living only for 'love, lust, and personal relationships', and men as putting love secondary to war, politics, duty and great public issues.
- interprets the play as the story of a great general betrayed by a treacherous strumpet, or as the triumph of transcendental love. Both views are sexist and over-simplify Shakespeare's play.
- demonstrates 'the most flagrant sexism' by demoting Cleopatra 'to the position of antagonist at best, nonentity at worst', making Antony the play's sole tragic protagonist.

Fitz also condemns male attitudes in the play itself. Enobarbus is 'a boringly conventional anti-feminist', and Roman values are exposed as unsavoury in the 'bride-bartering of Octavius and Antony, the cut-throat scramble for political ascendancy, and the unctuous hypocrisy of Octavius in the closing scenes'. Fitz' main endeavour is to insist that Cleopatra is equally the tragic hero of the play. She argues that Cleopatra feels fear and insecurity at the prospect of growing old ('wrinkled deep in time') and she 'has adopted measures to compensate, by being fascinating, for the ravages of age'. Cleopatra's full tragic status is confirmed by the fact that she 'learns and grows as Antony does not', and by Shakespeare's elevation of her to a more important role in the play than she has in Plutarch's *Lives*: raising her to the level of fully developed individuality, which qualifies her for treatment as a tragic figure . . . Shakespeare has taken pains to let Cleopatra explain her contrary behaviour and give reasons for it. He has created a complex but far from inscrutable being. Cleopatra's variety is, at last, finite. In short, Cleopatra needs to be demythologised. What she stands to lose in fascination, she stands to gain in humanity.

For Fitz, it is traditional male criticism that has mythologised and dehumanised Cleopatra into a dissembling, fickle, beguiling stereotype, a mere seductress. Her view is echoed by Juliet Dusinberre, who argues that in theatrical performances from 1847 productions have expressed current cultural attitudes towards powerful women, and that male reviewers have focused on the actress playing Cleopatra as 'the principal signifier of the anxieties and obsessions' of contemporary audiences. John Drakakis sees a similar 'male critical indulgence' at work in traditional criticism's eroticisation of Egypt, constructing it as extravagantly sensuous, self-indulgent and soft in contrast to Rome. Coppelia Kahn is similarly critical of the 'patriarchal gender ideology' that has demonised Cleopatra, as being both a woman and oriental. Such male prejudice results in the idea that 'the woman who holds or tries to hold political power will end by robbing the male of both political and sexual power'.

Kahn's book *Roman Shakespeare: Warriors, Wounds and Women* claims that Shakespeare's Roman plays 'articulate a critique of the ideology of gender'. She makes the point that gender (masculinity, feminity) is constructed, not something given at birth, and that in his Roman plays Shakespeare exposes how that construction takes place.

The relevance of Kahn's subtitle (*Warriors, Wounds and Women*) to *Antony and Cleopatra* is evident, and Kahn claims these three terms constitute 'Shakespeare's problematic of manly virtue'. 'Warriors' identifies the male rivalry ('emulation') that characterises the play, most obviously in the opposition of Antony and Caesar. 'Wounds', as in Antony's botched suicide attempt, are the physical, visible attributes of Roman virtue, and yet at the same time they signify the vulnerability associated with women. 'Women' are basic to the construction of males as Romans, mainly because they contrast with men by portraying opposing values. But in the play, Cleopatra threatens that fragile male identity. Kahn emphasises the fact that the staging of Cleopatra's suicide is exclusively a female affair, and that her suicide defeats Caesar in that it denies him the chance to exhibit her in triumph. Like Juliet, Cleopatra seizes on her 'power to die', and unlike Antony exploits it to the fullest:

> Finally as a spectacle executed with her elegant theatricality (no bungler she) and rich with imagistic suggestions of female fecundity and sensuality, her death seems to constitute a strong counterstatement to *virtus* (the Roman conception of manliness).

Feminist readings, like all critical interpretations, raise the question of whether they are what Shakespeare intended. Was he, as both Fitz and Kahn imply, submitting masculine values to dramatic critique and creating Cleopatra as a complex tragic hero? Whilst most critics today argue that Shakespeare's intentions can never be known, one distinctive feature of feminist criticism has become widely accepted: the play is as much Cleopatra's as Antony's; they are jointly the tragic heroes of the drama.

Performance criticism

Performance criticism fully acknowledges that *Antony and Cleopatra* is a play: a script to be performed by actors to an audience. It examines all aspects of the play in performance: its staging in the theatre or on film and video. Performance criticism focuses on Shakespeare's stagecraft and the semiotics of theatre (signs: words, costumes, gestures, etc.), together with the 'afterlife' of the play (what happened to *Antony and Cleopatra* after Shakespeare wrote it). That involves scrutiny of how productions at different periods have presented the play. As such, performance criticism appraises how the text has been cut, added to, rewritten and rearranged to present a version felt appropriate to the times.

Shakespeare probably wrote *Antony and Cleopatra* around 1606, but there is no record of a production in his lifetime. The play appeared in print for the first time in 1623 in the First Folio (see page 70), but for the next 200 years John Dryden's adaptation was much more popular than Shakespeare's original. First acted in 1678, Dryden's *All for Love, or, The World Well Lost* was written to suit the taste of the times which saw Shakespeare's play as sprawling and disordered, transgressing fashionable 'rules' of drama as it mixed tragedy with comedy and ranged widely over time and place.

Dryden's most obvious revision was to ensure that the play 'observed the unities'. The 'unities' is part of a theory of drama (based partly, but not entirely accurately, on the writings of the ancient Greek philosopher Aristotle) which states that, if a play is to possess aesthetic harmony, it must observe the unities of action, time and place. This means that it should have a single action lasting less than 24 hours, enacted in a single location. Dryden therefore sets the entire play in Alexandria, and the action takes place only during the last day of Antony and Cleopatra's lives.

Dryden's 'ordering' resulted in the marginalisation of the play's politics: Octavius does not appear, he is just an offstage presence, and Enobarbus disappears altogether. Cleopatra is much reduced, a far milder character; and Antony becomes the sole tragic protagonist as the play focuses, in a series of debate scenes, on his moral crisis. Dryden's version thus becomes a domestic rather than a political tragedy, and, as the subtitle suggests (*The World Well Lost*), Antony's choice of love is justified: he does not epitomise the folly of love in giving up an empire for a whore.

Well into the nineteenth century, Dryden's version held the stage, in spite of a brief unsuccessful attempt by David Garrick in 1759 to partly restore Shakespeare's play (with all the bawdy removed). In 1813, John Philip Kemble's production presented a heavily cut patchwork of Shakespeare and Dryden, as did William Charles Macready in 1833. These nineteenth-century productions set the trend for spectacular 'archaeological' stagings. Performances featured 'grand sea fights' with galleys on stage, funeral processions accompanied by large choirs, realistically painted scenery, and various parades, marches and festivities.

Only in 1849 was all of Dryden cut (together with much of Shakespeare), and that year's production further fed the taste for spectacle, which continued unabated for the rest of the century. Huge casts, victory processions, costumes modelled on the Roman and Egyptian antiquities in the British Museum and lavish 'Alexandrian revels' attempted to conjure up the Victorians' opulent conceptions of Rome and Egypt. An 1867 production featured Rome's Colosseum (which in reality was not built until 60 years after Cleopatra's death).

Other pageant-like productions featured Cleopatra in her state barge on the river of Cydnus as sumptuous animated tableaux, onstage galleys fighting the battle of Actium (with showers of arrows creating consternation among audiences), dancing girls on Pompey's galley, and other elaborate scenic effects.

After yet another spectacular production in 1907 (which began and ended with a vision of the Sphinx), the twentieth century saw a return to much simpler stagings. Productions no longer attempted to create an impression of realism. Under the influence of William Poel and Harley Granville-Barker, the stage was cleared of the clutter of historical detail. The aim was to recapture the conditions of the Elizabethan bare stage, which was not dependent on theatrical illusion. That implied a concern for the clear speaking of Shakespeare's language, a minimum of scenery, and scenes flowing swiftly into each other.

Such fluidity of stage movement characterises nearly all modern productions: scenes flow without break between Rome and Egypt, so making ironic contrasts clearer to audiences. Shakespeare's text is sometimes played in full, justifying Granville-Barker's claim that all 42 scenes can be successfully performed in sequence. Although occasional productions reduce the political aspects of the play, others have sought to exploit the political infighting to the full. For example, both the 1972 and 1978 Royal Shakespeare Company productions made much of the power politics of the play. The love interest was subordinated to the power struggle between Rome and Egypt and the factional disputes of Rome. But most modern productions continue to concentrate intensely on the love story, varying mainly in the emphasis they put on the political context within which it is set. And even in productions with minimal scenery, strenuous attempts are made to establish a striking contrast between Egypt and Rome: one a relaxed world of pleasure and ease, the other disciplined, constrained and militaristic.

A particularly valuable account of the performance history of the play is provided by Richard Madelaine (see page 127), which, like all such histories, reveals that no production has ever fully satisfied critics. The poetic power of the play, its contradictory central characters and its constantly shifting focus and setting, make demands that no single production, however inspired, can ever seem to fulfil.

Psychoanalytic criticism

In the twentieth century, psychoanalysis became a major influence on the understanding and interpretation of human behaviour. The founder of psychoanalysis, Sigmund Freud, explained personality as the result of unconscious and irrational desires, repressed memories or wishes, sexuality, fantasy, anxiety and conflict. Freud's theories have had a strong influence on the criticism and staging of Shakespeare's plays, most famously in the well-known claim that Hamlet suffers from an Oedipus complex.

Antony and Cleopatra, so concerned with its central characters' turbulent emotional relationship, has prompted attention from critics who adopt a psychoanalytic approach to Shakespeare's plays. Norman Holland, in *Psychoanalysis and Shakespeare,* records the following psychoanalytic interpretations:

- Antony and Cleopatra 'dying together' represents a common fantasy: the supreme consummation of love.
- The conflict of Rome and Egypt mirrors the conflicts in the two main characters 'who become at war with themselves'.
- Rome and Egypt represent different types of masculinity: Rome is a harsh fatherland where men are concerned only with aggression; in Egypt, masculinity means sexual submission to a female.
- Antony is trying to 'reach back towards an infant's total union with his nurturing mother'.
- The play represents a pagan memory of the death and rebirth of a sacrificial king, but through the deaths of Antony and Cleopatra, a Christian order is reaffirmed.
- The play reveals what Shakespeare was like: for example, he had an 'obsessive sexual fixation', he was like Enobarbus ('a man's man') and like Lepidus (not passing harsh judgements on characters).

Such interpretations reveal that psychoanalytic approaches are a specialised type of character criticism. They also demonstrate obvious weaknesses: they cannot be proved or disproved, and they are highly speculative. Psychoanalytic approaches are therefore often accused of imposing interpretations based on theory rather than on Shakespeare's text. But the play's evident interest in troubled relationships explains why many critics employ psychoanalytic concepts in their interpretations.

Postmodern criticism

Postmodern criticism (sometimes called 'deconstruction' or 'post-structuralism') is often difficult to understand because it is not centrally concerned with consistency or reasoned argument. It does not accept that one section of the story is necessarily connected to what follows, or that characters relate to each other in meaningful ways. The approach therefore has obvious drawbacks for examination students who are expected to display reasoned argument and respect for the evidence of the text.

Postmodern approaches to *Antony and Cleopatra* are most clearly seen in stage productions. There, you could think of it as simply 'a mixture of styles'. The label 'postmodern' is applied to productions which selfconsciously show little regard for consistency in character or for coherence in telling the story. Characters are dressed in costumes from very different historical periods.

Postmodern criticism most typically revels in the cleverness of its own use of language, and accepts all kinds of anomalies and contradictions in a spirit of playfulness or 'carnival'. Some postmodern critics even deny the possibility of finding meaning in language. They claim that words simply refer to other words, and so any interpretation is endlessly delayed. Antony himself seems to indulge in such postmodern playfulness as he impresses the gullible Lepidus with his meaningless description of the crocodile:

> It is shaped, sir, like itself, and it is as broad as it hath breadth. It is just so high as it is, and moves with it own organs. It lives by that which nourisheth it, and the elements once out of it, it transmigrates.   *(Act 2 Scene 7, lines 38–41)*

Antony and Cleopatra has attracted little postmodern criticism in spite of its contradictory, unstable nature. Terry Eagleton, for example, employs a mixture of political, feminist and character approaches:

> What deconstructs political order in the play is desire, and the figure for this is Cleopatra. In predictably patriarchal style, Cleopatra is portrayed as capricious and self-contradictory, undoing all coherence in her exasperating inconsistency. She is, as it were, pure heterogeneity, an 'infinite variety' that eludes any stable position.

Organising your responses

The purpose of this section is to help you improve your writing about *Antony and Cleopatra*. It offers practical guidance on two kinds of tasks: writing about an extract from the play and writing an essay. Whether you are answering an examination question, preparing coursework (term papers), or carrying out research into your own chosen topic, this section will help you organise and present your responses.

In all your writing, there are three vital things to remember:

- *Antony and Cleopatra* is a play. Although it is usually referred to as a 'text', *Antony and Cleopatra* is not a book, but a script intended to be acted on a stage. So your writing should demonstrate an awareness of the play in performance as theatre. That means you should always try to read the play with an 'inner eye', thinking about how it could look and sound on stage. The next best thing to seeing an actual production is to imagine yourself sitting in the audience, watching and listening to *Antony and Cleopatra* being performed. By doing so, you will be able to write effectively about Shakespeare's language and dramatic techniques.
- *Antony and Cleopatra* is not a presentation of 'reality'. It is a dramatic construct in which the playwright, through theatre, engages the emotions and intellect of the audience. The characters and story may persuade an audience to suspend its disbelief for several hours. The audience may identify with the characters, be deeply moved by them, and may think of them as if they are living human beings. However, when you write, a major part of your task is to show how Shakespeare achieves his dramatic effects that so engage the audience. Through discussion of his handling of language, character and plot, your writing reveals how Shakespeare uses themes and ideas, attitudes and values, to give insight into crucial social, moral and political dilemmas of his time – and yours.
- How Shakespeare learned his craft. As a schoolboy, and in his early years as a dramatist, Shakespeare used all kinds of models or frameworks to guide his writing. But he quickly learned how to vary and adapt the models to his own dramatic purposes. This

section offers frameworks that you can use to structure your writing. As you use them, follow Shakespeare's example! Adapt them to suit your own writing style and needs.

Writing about an extract

It is an expected part of all Shakespeare study that you should be able to write well about an extract (sometimes called a 'passage') from the play. An extract is usually between 30 and 70 lines long, and you are invited to comment on it. The instructions vary. Sometimes the task is very briefly expressed:

- Write a detailed commentary on the following passage.
- Write about the effect of the extract on your own thoughts and feelings.

At other times a particular focus is specified for your writing:

- With close reference to the language and imagery of the passage, show in what ways it helps to establish important issues in the play.
- Analyse the style and structure of the extract, showing what it contributes to your appreciation of the play's major concerns.

In writing your response, you must of course take account of the precise wording of the task and ensure you concentrate on each particular point specified. But however the invitation to write about an extract is expressed, it requires you to comment in detail on the language. You should identify and evaluate how the language reveals character, contributes to plot development, offers opportunities for dramatic effect, and embodies crucial concerns of the play as a whole. These 'crucial concerns' are also referred to as the 'themes', or 'issues', or 'preoccupations' of the play.

The following framework is a guide to how you can write a detailed commentary on an extract. Writing a paragraph or more on each item will help you bring out the meaning and significance of the extract and show how Shakespeare achieves his effects.

> **Paragraph 1:** Locate the extract in the play and say who is on stage.
> **Paragraph 2:** State what the extract is about and identify its structure.
> **Paragraph 3:** Identify the mood or atmosphere of the extract.
> **Paragraphs 4–8:**
>   Diction (vocabulary)
>   Imagery
>   Antithesis
>   Repetition
>   Lists
> } These paragraphs analyse how Shakespeare achieves his effects. They concentrate on the language of the extract, showing the dramatic effect of each item, and how the language expresses crucial concerns of the play.
> **Paragraph 9:** Staging opportunities
> **Paragraph 10:** Conclusion

The analysis and examples of different types of language used by Shakespeare (imagery, antithesis, etc.) on pages 82–91 will help you in constructing your own response. The following example uses the framework to show how the paragraphs making up the essay might be written. The framework headings (in bold), would not of course appear in your essay. They are presented only to help you see how the framework is used. The extract is from Act 4 Scene 15, lines 43–96. (You will also find it helpful to read how the passage is discussed in the Commentary, pages 57–8.)

ANTONY I am dying, Egypt, dying.
     Give me some wine, and let me speak a little.
CLEOPATRA No, let me speak, and let me rail so high
     That the false huswife Fortune break her wheel,
     Provoked by my offence.
ANTONY   One word, sweet queen: 5
     Of Caesar seek your honour, with your safety. O!
CLEOPATRA They do not go together.
ANTONY   Gentle, hear me.
     None about Caesar trust but Proculeius.
CLEOPATRA My resolution and my hands I'll trust,
     None about Caesar.   10
ANTONY The miserable change now at my end
     Lament nor sorrow at, but please your thoughts
     In feeding them with those my former fortunes,
     Wherein I lived the greatest prince o'th'world,

The noblest; and do now not basely die,   15
        Not cowardly put off my helmet to
        My countryman – a Roman by a Roman
        Valiantly vanquished. Now my spirit is going;
        I can no more.
CLEOPATRA   Noblest of men, woo't die?
        Hast thou no care of me? Shall I abide   20
        In this dull world, which in thy absence is
        No better than a sty? O see, my women:
                                        [Antony dies]
        The crown o'th'earth doth melt. My lord!
        O, withered is the garland of the war;
        The soldier's pole is fall'n! Young boys and girls   25
        Are level now with men; the odds is gone,
        And there is nothing left remarkable
        Beneath the visiting moon. [She starts to faint]
CHARMIAN O, quietness, lady!
IRAS She's dead too, our sovereign.   30
CHARMIAN Lady!
IRAS Madam!
CHARMIAN O madam, madam, madam!
IRAS Royal Egypt! Empress!   [Cleopatra stirs]
CHARMIAN Peace, peace, Iras.   35
CLEOPATRA No more but e'en a woman, and commanded
        By such poor passion as the maid that milks
        And does the meanest chares. It were for me
        To throw my sceptre at the injurious gods,
        To tell them that this world did equal theirs   40
        Till they had stol'n our jewel. All's but naught;
        Patience is sottish, and impatience does
        Become a dog that's mad. Then is it sin
        To rush into the secret house of death
        Ere death dare come to us? How do you, women?   45
        What, what, good cheer! Why, how now, Charmian?
        My noble girls! Ah, women, women! Look,
        Our lamp is spent, it's out. Good sirs, take heart.
        We'll bury him; and then, what's brave, what's noble,
        Let's do't after the high Roman fashion   50
        And make death proud to take us. Come, away.

This case of that huge spirit now is cold.
Ah, women, women! Come, we have no friend
But resolution and the briefest end.

Paragraph 1: Locate the extract in the play and identify who is on stage

Antony, defeated by Caesar and believing Cleopatra is dead, has attempted suicide. Mortally wounded, but learning that Cleopatra lives, he has ordered his guards to take him to her. Now Cleopatra, Charmian and Iras have hauled him up into the monument where Cleopatra has welcomed him with a kiss. The women and Antony are alone on stage.

Paragraph 2: State what the extract is about and identify its structure

(Begin with one or two sentences identifying what the extract is about, followed by several sentences briefly identifying its structure, that is, the unfolding events and the different sections of the extract.)

The extract dramatises Antony's dying moments and Cleopatra's reaction to his death. Antony beseeches Cleopatra to find honour and safety with Caesar, and to trust only Proculeius. His final words entreat her not to grieve, but to rejoice in memories of his former greatness. He dies, certain that his death is noble. Cleopatra is grief-stricken and mourns that his death deprives the world of all distinction. She faints, but revives and claims she is merely a woman, moved by the same feelings as the most lowly female. Thinking Antony's death makes everything meaningless, she decides on suicide, and cheers her women with the assurance of the nobility of the deed. Death will be proud to take them.

Paragraph 3: Identify the mood or atmosphere of the extract

The heightened atmosphere of the whole extract is appropriate to its subject matter: the death of a tragic hero. But from moment to moment there are distinct shifts of mood. The opening is poignant as Antony struggles desperately to advise Cleopatra and she barely listens. She expresses rage against Fortune and herself, sardonically questions Caesar's honour, and seems to reject Antony's advice to trust Proculeius. In contrast, Antony's dying speech achieves sad and tragic dignity as he forbids sorrow, urges Cleopatra to remember his former glory, and asserts the nobility of his death. But an undercurrent of dramatic irony also pervades his words, because the play has shown him often acting ignobly. Cleopatra's lament powerfully conveys her desolation, and is followed by a brief, panic-filled episode as her women fear she is dead. Reviving, her changing emotions successively express calm humility, defiance, forlorn resignation ('All's but naught . . . mad'), then determination as she resolves on death and cheers her women. Her final seven lines convey the self-assurance of a tragic hero unafraid to die.

Paragraph 4: Diction (vocabulary)

Although the imagery is complex, and the extract is characterised by the elevated tone of tragedy, few words are unfamiliar. 'Huswife' was the Jacobean contraction of 'housewife' (but also could imply 'hussy' or harlot), 'woo't' was 'wouldst thou', 'sty' implies pigsty, 'odds' means 'distinction' or difference, 'meanest chares' are 'most lowly chores', 'sottish' is 'foolish', and 'sirs' was sometimes used to address women in Shakespeare's time. Elsewhere, suicide is variously alluded to as 'My resolution and my hands', to 'not basely die', to 'rush into the secret house of death', 'the high Roman fashion', and 'resolution and the briefest end'. And the tragic atmosphere is reinforced throughout by ordinary words or expressions which balance loss against gain, and defeat against endurance or transcendence: for example, 'Lament' and 'sorrow' versus 'Valiantly vanquished'; 'withered' and 'naught' versus 'good cheer' and 'make death proud'.

Paragraph 5: Imagery

Vivid images in the passage are reminders of imagery and themes that run through the play. Cleopatra imagines Antony and herself at the lowest point of the wheel of fortune, using personification as she rails against 'the false huswife Fortune'. The theme of change is even more tellingly depicted in Cleopatra's lament over the dead Antony. It begins with one of the many images of melting that run through the play, picturing Antony as the earth's dissolving crown. She then imagines him as a shrivelled victory wreath, and her expression 'The soldier's pole is fall'n!' conjures up a wealth of associations: a broken spear, a military standard carried before troops into battle, a fallen polestar which once guided everyone, a lifeless phallus, a broken maypole (echoing 'garland'). Her final image suggests that all distinction ('odds') has vanished with Antony's death; nothing on earth ('Beneath the visiting moon') has any uniqueness or merit.

The images in Cleopatra's last speech create a variety of effects. For example, the simile she uses to compare her feelings to those of a mere milkmaid expresses a brief moment of newfound humility. Her grief makes her rage that she will throw her sceptre at the gods for stealing Antony ('our jewel'), which is an example of the play's cosmic imagery, here hyperbolically establishing the lovers' world as equal to the gods'. Death is depicted in several striking images: 'the secret house', 'Our lamp is spent', 'the high Roman fashion' (suicide) which will make death 'proud' to take Cleopatra and her women, and 'the briefest end'. Such images convey Cleopatra's complex emotions in facing death and intensify the tragedy of the scene.

Paragraph 6: Antithesis
The conflict that characterises the entire play finds subtle expression in the antitheses in the passage. Even at this tragic moment, echoes of the lovers' constant wrangling surface in Antony's 'let me speak a little', followed instantly by Cleopatra's 'No, let me speak'. The opposition of Egypt and Rome is ironically acknowledged in Cleopatra's recognition that 'honour' and 'safety' are incompatible if she submits to Caesar. Antony's dying speech uses antithesis as he urges not 'sorrow', but thoughts that 'please'. Those pleasing thoughts are that he is 'The noblest', and does not 'basely die', not 'cowardly' but 'Valiantly vanquished'. Similar antitheses, sustaining Antony's and Cleopatra's constant concern to portray themselves as heroic lovers, continue in Cleopatra's lament where Antony's former glory is set against his death: 'crown' versus 'melt', 'withered' versus 'garland', and so on. And in her final speech, that loss is devastatingly expressed in the bleak antithesis of 'All's but naught'. But Cleopatra stoically sets 'Patience' against 'impatience' and rejects both to choose suicide. Without Antony, their only 'friend' is death itself: 'the briefest end'.

Paragraph 7: Repetition
The repetition of certain words heightens dramatic effect. Antony's 'I am dying, Egypt, dying' has an urgency that conveys he knows he has only a short time in which to speak his last words to Cleopatra. Charmian's 'O madam, madam, madam!' has similar urgency, but here reveals her fear that her mistress is dead. Cleopatra's 'Peace, peace' is in quite a different emotional register, and serves to

introduce a humble admission of her common humanity. Antony's alliterative 'a Roman by a Roman / Valiantly vanquished', reinforced by the measured rhythm of his verse, helps create an impression of confidence and stoicism befitting a tragic hero. His heroic status is subtly reinforced by the recurrence of the words 'noblest' and 'noble'. Perhaps the most effective repetition occurs as the scene draws to its close: Cleopatra's repetition of 'women' echoes the final stage picture and unites the women in a sisterhood of comfort and determination for death.

Paragraph 8: Lists
Shakespeare's technique of piling item on item in a list is evident in Cleopatra's lament as she accumulates striking images to convey the devastating effects of Antony's death. Each image adds to the sense of loss, and the sequence culminates in the desolation of 'nothing left remarkable / Beneath the visiting moon': a vision of a world without individuality or excellence. There are no obvious 'word lists' in the extract. Instead, Shakespeare seems to use a 'doubling' effect. Paired words or expressions intensify meaning and emotional impact: 'My resolution and my hands', 'Lament nor sorrow', 'what's brave, what's noble', 'resolution and the briefest end'.

Paragraph 9: Staging opportunities
The extract offers opportunities for thrilling theatrical presentation. The stage focus is tight and there is little movement. The three women group around the dying Antony, and Cleopatra holds him in a way which expresses her love, grief and desolation. Antony's final speech offers scope for the actor to achieve a nobility in dying that has often been absent from his conduct in the play. Even more powerfully, Shakespeare provides Cleopatra with the finest poetry in which to express her sense of emptiness and loss. Words, rather than action, have the most dramatic effect here. Cleopatra's fainting creates a brief flurry of action, but, again, Charmian and Iras are almost certainly more dramatically effective if the grouping is kept tight and their anxiety is conveyed through their words. Only part way through the final speech do the women begin to move, as Cleopatra, intent on suicide, cheers her women. On 'Come, away', they prepare to carry off Antony's body in a way which underlines their dignity and determination.

Paragraph 10: Conclusion

The extract shows Antony and Cleopatra as tragic heroes. He dies nobly and she bravely prepares for her own death. But Shakespeare allows a more ironic interpretation: the extract can also be read as the two lovers continuing to construct their own myth of themselves as extraordinary, epic figures. Antony's advice to trust Proculeius later proves unwise as Proculeius captures Cleopatra. His claim not to die 'basely', but 'Valiantly vanquished' is undercut both by his botched suicide attempt, and by Cleopatra's second desertion in battle. Similarly, Cleopatra's mourning can be seen as yet more of the hyperbolic illusion that characterises the play. And her decision to commit suicide is called into question in Act 5: it is the prospect of being led in Caesar's triumph that really makes her resolve to die. Nonetheless, even in this brief extract, much of her 'infinite variety' is evident in her swiftly changing moods.

Reminders

- The framework is only a guide. It helps you to structure your writing. Use the framework for practice on other extracts. Adapt it as you feel appropriate. Make it your own.
- Structure your response in paragraphs. Each paragraph makes a particular point and helps build up your argument.
- Focus tightly on the language, especially vocabulary, imagery, antithesis, lists, repetitions.
- Remember that *Antony and Cleopatra* is a play, a drama intended for performance. The purpose of writing about an extract is to identify how Shakespeare creates dramatic effect. What techniques does he use?
- Try to imagine the action. Visualise the scene in your mind's eye. But remember there can be many valid ways of performing a scene. Offer alternatives. Justify your own preferences by reference to the language.
- Who is on stage? Imagine their interaction. How do 'silent characters' react to what is said?
- Look for the theatrical qualities of the extract. What guides for actors' movement and expressions are given in the language? Comment on any stage directions.
- How might the audience respond? In Jacobean times? Today?

How might you respond as a member of the audience?
- How might the lines be spoken? Tone, emphasis, pace, pauses? Identify shifting moods and registers. What are the characteristics of the verse or prose (see page 91)?
- What is the importance of the extract in the play as a whole? Justify its thematic significance.
- Are there 'key words'?
- How does the extract develop the plot, reveal character, deepen themes?
- Offer a variety of interpretations.

Writing an essay

As part of your study of *Antony and Cleopatra*, you will be asked to write essays, either under examination conditions or for coursework (term papers). Examinations mean that you are under pressure of time, usually having around one hour to prepare and write each essay. Coursework means that you have much longer to think about and produce your essay. But, whatever the type of essay, each will require you to develop an argument about a particular aspect of *Antony and Cleopatra*.

Before suggesting a strategy for your essay-writing, it is helpful to recall just what an essay is. Essay comes from the French *essai*: to attempt, or to make a trial. It was originally used by the sixteenth-century French writer Montaigne (whose work Shakespeare certainly read). Montaigne used *essais* to attempt to find out what he thought about particular subjects, such as friendship, or cannibals, or education. In each essay he used many practical examples to test his response to the topic.

The essays you write on *Antony and Cleopatra* similarly require that you set out your thoughts on a particular aspect of the play, using evidence from the text. The people who read your essays (examiners, teachers, lecturers) will have certain expectations of your writing. In each essay they will expect you to discuss and analyse a particular topic, using evidence from the play to develop an argument in an organised, coherent and persuasive way. Examiners look for, and reward, what they call 'an informed personal response'. This simply means that you show you have good knowledge of the play ('informed') and can use evidence from it to support and justify your own viewpoint ('personal').

You can write about *Antony and Cleopatra* from different points of view. As pages 96–107 show, you can approach the play from a number of critical perspectives (political, psychoanalytic, feminist, etc.). You can also set the play in its social, literary, political and other contexts, as shown on pages 70–81. You should write at different levels, moving beyond description to analysis and evaluation. Simply telling the story or describing characters is not as effective as analysing how events or characters embody wider concerns of the play: its themes, issues and preoccupations. In your writing, always give practical examples (quotations, actions) which illustrate the themes you discuss.

How should you answer an examination question or write a coursework essay? The following threefold structure can help you organise your response:

> opening paragraph
> developing paragraphs
> concluding paragraph.

Opening paragraph Begin with a paragraph identifying just what topic or issue you will focus on. Show that you have understood what the question is about. You probably will have prepared for particular topics. But look closely at the question and identify key words to see what particular aspect it asks you to write about. Adapt your material to answer that question. Examiners do not reward an essay, however well-written, if it is not on the question set.

Developing paragraphs This is the main body of your essay. In it, you develop your argument, point by point, paragraph by paragraph. Use evidence from the play that illuminates the topic or issue and answers the question set. Each paragraph should make a point of dramatic or thematic significance. Some paragraphs could make points concerned with context or particular critical approaches. The effect of your argument builds up as each paragraph adds to the persuasive quality of your essay. Use brief quotations that support your argument, and show clearly just why they are relevant. Ensure that your essay demonstrates that you are aware that *Antony and Cleopatra* is a play, a drama intended for performance, and therefore open to a wide variety of interpretations and audience response.

Concluding paragraph Your final paragraph pulls together your main conclusions. It does not simply repeat what you have written earlier, but summarises concisely how your essay has successfully answered the question.

Example

Question: Discuss the view that 'The many contrasts in the play derive from the opposition of the values of Rome and Egypt'.

The following notes show the 'ingredients' of an answer. In an examination it is usually helpful to prepare similar notes from which you write your essay, paragraph by paragraph. To help you understand how contextual matters or points from different critical approaches might be included, the words 'Context' or 'Criticism' appear before some items. Remember that examiners are not impressed by 'name-dropping': use of critics' names. What they want you to show is your knowledge and judgement of the play and its contexts, and of how it has been interpreted from different critical perspectives.

Opening paragraph

Show you are aware that the question asks you to identify the contrasts in the play and to discuss how far they derive from the opposition of Roman and Egyptian values. So identify those values, note the contrasts you propose to discuss (establish a simple framework to structure your answer) and say you will give your view on how far you think they derive from the Rome–Egypt opposition. Also show that you are aware that the question asks you to give a response to a 'view' – and views are always disputable! So include the following points and aim to write a sentence or more on each:

- The most obvious contrast in the play is that between Rome and Egypt. Rome values order, control, obedience and military glory. Egypt values leisure, extravagance, hedonism and love.

- But the play contains many other contrasts, for example of character, events, language and themes.
- How far these contrasts 'derive' from the Rome–Egypt opposition is questionable. Some seem to arise directly from it, but with others the nature of the relationship is more problematic.
- This essay will therefore discuss certain major contrasts, and judge how far each might derive from the Rome–Egypt opposition.

Developing paragraphs

Now write a paragraph or more on each of the following contrasts:

- *Antony versus Caesar* <mark>Criticism: political</mark> Caesar is austere, calculating and Machiavellian; Antony is passionate, impulsive and driven by his desire for Cleopatra. Caesar is enslaved to his public duty as triumvir; Antony is enslaved to love. Each man thus represents Roman or Egyptian values (e.g. Caesar's condemnation of Antony's 'lascivious wassails'). But both men are equally committed to the Roman values of military success and conquest: their opposition is as much based on shared Roman values as on Antony's differing Egyptian values. For example, Antony's suicide derives from his Roman commitment ('a Roman by a Roman / Valiantly vanquished').
- *Antony's past versus his present* <mark>Criticism: traditional and political</mark> The play continually contrasts Antony's heroic past with his tarnished present (expressed in the Roman Philo's view of Antony's 'Egyptian' behaviour: 'The triple pillar of the world transformed / Into a strumpet's fool'). Once he was a Mars or Hercules, now his enchantment by Cleopatra has weakened and debauched him. His decline can be seen as Roman values yielding to Egyptian. But a too-simple contrast of past and present overlooks how Antony still retains many Roman qualities: political will, concern for nobility, bravery in battle. And his gratuitously cruel treatment of Thidias derives from a distortion of both Roman and Egyptian values, not their opposition.
- *Cleopatra's 'infinite variety'* <mark>Criticism: feminist</mark> The contradictions of Cleopatra's behaviour, her wildly swinging emotions, her delight in tormenting Antony and her uncontrolled grief for him, her pettiness and nobility, cannot be reduced simply to the opposition of Egyptian and Roman values: wilfulness versus integrity. The play provides many Roman (male) condemnations of her

('strumpet', 'gipsy', etc.), but the sheer range of her emotions and actions, together with her determination to die in 'the high Roman fashion', go beyond a contrast of Roman and Egyptian values, combining and exceeding them.

- *Love versus lust* Criticism: traditional Neither Egyptian nor Roman values can fully encompass differing interpretations of the nature of Antony and Cleopatra's love. The play's Romans see it as no more than lasciviousness or enchantment, the Egyptians as an exalted love affair. But neither Roman nor Egyptian values as expressed in the play can contain the lovers' final transcendent vision of themselves as achieving immortal union in death.

- *Contrasting events* Criticism Caesar ends the play speaking of 'High events'. But the play contains a huge range of contrasting events: a great battle ends in ignoble flight; a clown lectures a queen; a political conference is followed by a drunken party; women laugh together as their fortunes are told, but die in dignity; a great warrior botches his suicide; Cleopatra resolutely determines to die, but shortly after lies to Caesar about her wealth; the lyrical description of her majestic appearance at Cydnus contrasts with her beating of the messenger and her obsessive jealousy of Octavia; she plays wilfully with Antony's emotions but mourns him in sublime lament. The play's mixture of the commonplace and the cosmic, grandeur and farce, heroism and anticlimax, owes less to the opposing values of Rome and Egypt than to Shakespeare's dramatic skill in juxtaposing comedy with tragedy, heroism with human fallibility.

- *Contrasts of language* At first sight, the language of the play seems to derive from the opposition of values. Roman speech appears measured and sternly economic; Egyptian speech seems convivial, sensual, exaggerated. But these distinctions are stereotypes, and what both Roman and Egyptian speakers share is the construction of illusions that sustain the worlds and values they desire. Caesar praises Antony's past greatness; Cleopatra dreams of him as superhuman hero. But Ventidius exposes the gap between the rhetoric and reality of Roman military virtue, and Dolabella's 'Gentle madam, no' undercuts Cleopatra's hyperbolic praise of Antony.

Concluding paragraph

Write several sentences pulling together your conclusions. You might include the following points:

- At first sight, the view that the play's contrasts all derive from the opposition of the values of Rome and Egypt seems plausible. For example, Rome seems a public, political world; Egypt, private and emotional.
- Context and Criticism: political But the claim is highly contestable and has its roots in traditional contrasts of Shakespeare's time: of European values versus those of the Orient or the newly discovered word of the Americas. Roman and Egyptian values are not as clear-cut as they seem, and their opposition diminishes the complexity of Shakespeare's dramatisation. Neither characters, plot, nor themes can be reduced to simple explanations of cause and effect. Egypt is 'political' as well as 'personal'.
- Other contrasts such as loyalty versus betrayal, masculinity versus femininity, similarly depend on stereotyping.
- The play frequently dissolves contrasts and oppositions in images of melting and dissolution. Like Caesar's 'vagabond flag' or Antony's constantly mutating cloud shapes, identity, events and desires are constantly in motion. To 'fix' them in critical categories undermines the ever-changing nature of the play.

Writing about character

Much critical writing about *Antony and Cleopatra* traditionally focused on characters, writing about them as if they were living human beings. Today it is not sufficient just to describe their personalities. When you write about characters you will also be expected to show that they are dramatic constructs, part of Shakespeare's stagecraft. They embody the wider concerns of the play, have certain dramatic functions, and are set in a social and political world with particular values and beliefs. They reflect and express issues of significance to Shakespeare's society – and today's.

Of course you should say what a character seems like to you, but you should also write about how Shakespeare makes him or her part of his overall dramatic design. But there is a danger in writing about the functions of characters or the character types they represent. To reduce a character to a mere plot device is just as inappropriate as treating him or her as a real person. When you write about characters you should therefore try to achieve a balance between analysing their personalities, identifying the dilemmas they face, and placing them in their social, critical and dramatic contexts. And the basic material for that is in the text: what the characters say, what they do, and what others say about them.

For example, Cleopatra is endlessly discussed or described by other characters. Enobarbus speaks of her 'infinite variety'. For Antony, she can be an 'enchanting queen' or 'foul Egyptian'; for Charmian, a 'lass unparalleled'; for Caesar, 'dear queen' to her face and 'whore' behind her back. Her actions and words display a similarly mercurial range: bravery and cowardice, cruelty and gentleness. Taunting mockery, deviousness, jealousy, capriciousness, pride, self-indulgence and humility are only a fraction of her 'infinite variety'. At the end of the play she achieves a kind of splendour in her suicide as she strives to fulfil her immortal longings: a reunion with Antony, transcending death itself. It may be an illusion, yet another of the grandiose fantasies she constructs of herself and Antony, but it is thrillingly theatrical, and a dramatically satisfying climax to the rollercoasting emotional ride on which she has taken the audience.

For Jacobeans, Cleopatra embodied historical conceptions of the Egyptian queen. For Victorians, she was the sterotypical vision of the oriental *femme fatale*, breathing sensuality, and utterly unreliable. For the modern critic Arnold Kettle, she possesses 'an immense talent for provocation'. But for many feminist critics, she is a wily politician, using all her considerable skills and charm to retain control of her country, and when that endeavour fails, exercising her independence in choosing death rather than humiliation. In her paradoxical behaviour, they see the complex strategies of a woman who has to live and survive in a male, militaristic world.

In creating Cleopatra, Shakespeare offers every reader and audience member many opportunities to reflect on such themes as the nature of love, the exercise of power in personal and political relationships, and the conflicts that ensue in such relationships. Her endless game-playing, self-dramatisation and image-management raise crucial questions about a theme that every Shakespeare play explores: what reality lies behind outward appearance? Perhaps most strikingly of all, Cleopatra's 'infinite variety' exemplifies that other common Shakespearian theme: change. The play's constant movement, its transformations and shifting fortunes, its recurring images of melting and dissolution, find their reflection in Cleopatra's mercurial nature, and in her final attempt to transcend earthly bonds and achieve immortal union with Antony.

A note on examiners

Examiners do not try to trap you or trick you. They set questions and select passages for comment intended to help you write your own informed personal response to the play. They expect your answer to display a sound knowledge and understanding of the play, and to be well structured. They want you to develop an argument, using evidence from the text to support your interpretations and judgements. Examiners know there is never one 'right answer' to a question, but always opportunities to explore different approaches and interpretations. As such, they welcome answers which directly address the question set, and which demonstrate originality, insight and awareness of complexity. Above all, they reward responses which show your perception that *Antony and Cleopatra* is a play for performance and that you can identify how Shakespeare achieves his dramatic effects.

And what about critics? Examiners want you to show you are aware of different critical approaches to the play. But they do not expect you simply to drop critics' names into your essay, or to remember quotations from critics. Rather, they want you to show that you can interpret the play from different critical perspectives, and that you know that any critical approach provides only a partial view of *Antony and Cleopatra*. Often, that need only be just a section of your essay. Examiners are always interested in your view of the play. They expect your writing to show how you have come to that view from thinking critically about the play, reading it, reading about it, seeing it performed, and perhaps from acting some of it yourself – even if that acting is in your imagination!

Resources

Books

Janet Adelman, *The Common Liar*, Yale University Press, 1973
A detailed examination of the verse of the play. Adelman argues that 'we can neither believe nor wholly disbelieve the claims made by the poetry'. Adelman's chapter 'Nature's Piece 'gainst Fancy: Poetry and the Structure of Belief in *Antony and Cleopatra*' is reprinted in John Drakakis (ed.), *New Casebooks: Antony and Cleopatra, Contemporary Critical Essays*, Macmillan, 1994.

A C Bradley, *Oxford Lectures on Poetry*, Oxford University Press, 1905
The chapter 'Shakespeare's *Antony and Cleopatra*' questions whether the play is a tragedy, and is critical of its dramatic structure. It is reprinted in John Russell Brown (ed.), *Shakespeare: Antony and Cleopatra, A Casebook*, Macmillan, 1968.

John Russell Brown (ed.), *Shakespeare: Antony and Cleopatra, A Casebook*, Macmillan, 1968
Contains a valuable collection of critical writing on *Antony and Cleopatra* from 1678 to 1966, including that by Bradley and Charney noted in this booklist.

Maurice Charney, *Shakespeare's Roman Plays: The Function of Imagery in the Drama*, Harvard University Press, 1961
Charney's chapter 'The imagery of *Antony and Cleopatra*' is reprinted in John Russell Brown (ed.), *Shakespeare: Antony and Cleopatra, A Casebook*, Macmillan, 1968.

W H Clemen, *The Development of Shakespeare's Imagery*, 2nd edition, Methuen, 1977
The chapter on *Antony and Cleopatra* notes the special importance of the play's 'Egyptian' images (the Nile, serpents, etc.), and its 'light' images (stars, moon, sun) that presage Antony's fall.

John F Danby, *Poets on Fortune's Hill*, Faber and Faber, 1952
Danby sees the play as a dialectic of opposites which merge, unite and fall apart; and as Shakespeare's 'adjustment to the new Jacobean tastes', particularly the interest in the myth of Mars and Venus. Danby's chapter '*Antony and Cleopatra*: A Shakespearian adjustment' is reprinted in John Drakakis (ed.), *New Casebooks: Antony and Cleopatra, Contemporary Critical Essays*, Macmillan, 1994.

H Neville Davies, 'Jacobean *Antony and Cleopatra*', in John Drakakis (ed.), *New Casebooks: Antony and Cleopatra, Contemporary Critical Essays*, Macmillan, 1994
Argues that Shakespeare partly based his portrayals of Caesar and Antony on King James I and King Christian IV of Denmark respectively.

Jonathan Dollimore, *Radical Tragedy*, revised edition, Harvester Wheatsheaf, 1989
In this 'cultural materialism' (political) approach, Dollimore locates Shakespeare's tragedies in the context of their times, and interprets *Antony and Cleopatra* as concerned with social and political relations in which Antony's honour derives from Rome's power structure.

John Drakakis (ed.), *New Casebooks: Antony and Cleopatra, Contemporary Critical Essays*, Macmillan, 1994
A valuable collection of modern criticism (contains articles by Adelman, Danby, Davies and Fitz noted in this booklist).

Juliet Dusinberre, 'Squeaking Cleopatras: Gender and Performance in *Antony and Cleopatra*', in James C Bulman (ed.), *Shakespeare: Theory, and Performance*, Routledge, 1996
A feminist reading which argues that 'Cleopatra, as performer and critic of performance, is always in control of her own play: in control of Antony, of her own image-making, and of the audience'.

Terry Eagleton, *William Shakespeare*, Basil Blackwell, 1986
Eagleton includes only a very short section on *Antony and Cleopatra*, but his combination of political, feminist and postmodern (or deconstructive) approaches suggests how the play dramatises contradiction and instability.

Linda Fitz, 'Egyptian Queens and Male Reviewers: Sexist Attitudes in *Antony and Cleopatra* Criticism', in John Drakakis (ed.), *New Casebooks: Antony and Cleopatra, Contemporary Critical Essays*, Macmillan, 1994
A very readable feminist essay which launches an all-out attack on traditional criticism as sexist, and argues for the full tragic status of Cleopatra.

Harley Granville-Barker, *Prefaces to Shakespeare*: Antony and Cleopatra, Batsford, 1930
Granville-Barker stoutly defends the play's dramatic construction.

Margot Heinemann, '"Let Rome in Tiber melt": Order and Disorder in *Antony and Cleopatra*', in John Drakakis (ed.), *New Casebooks: Antony and Cleopatra, Contemporary Critical Essays*, Macmillan, 1994
Argues that the passionate love portrayed in the play is inseparable from the politics: the struggle for control of Egypt and the world. Also identifies

the political riskiness of the play's subject matter in Jacobean times.

Coppelia Kahn, *Roman Shakespeare: Warriors, Wounds and Women*, Taylor and Francis, 1996
A feminist study of Shakespeare's Roman plays that explores the gender ideologies behind 'Roman virtue'. Stresses the male rivaly ('emulation') in *Antony and Cleopatra*, and argues that 'Shakespeare reconstructs his heroine as a Roman wife allowed just enough autonomy to choose death as testament of her love for her husband'.

Frank Kermode, *Shakespeare's Language*, Allen Lane, Penguin, 2000
A detailed examination of how Shakespeare's language changed over the course of his playwriting career. Contains a helpful section on *Antony and Cleopatra*.

Arnold Kettle, *'Antony and Cleopatra'*, in Kiernan Ryan (ed.), *Shakespeare: Texts and Contexts*, Macmillan, 2000
A valuable introduction that argues powerfully against seeing the play in terms of such simple oppositions as Rome versus Egypt, or politics versus love. Kettle's essay is followed by a helpful review of recent criticism of the play: 'Changing critical perspectives' by Cicely Palser Havely.

Victor Kiernan, *Eight Tragedies of Shakespeare: A Marxist Study*, Verso, 1996
Argues that Shakespeare's personal experience is expressed in his plays as sympathy for the poor. For Kiernan, the tragic world of *Antony and Cleopatra* 'lies between an old social and moral order and a newer one . . . clothed in the guise of East and West'.

G Wilson Knight, *The Imperial Theme*, Taylor and Francis, 1965
Shakespeare's Roman plays are interpreted through cosmic images, symbolism and themes. Knight's interpretations of *Antony and Cleopatra* as 'Transcendental Humanism' and 'The Diadem of Love' are today regarded as hyperbolic, but are still well worth reading.

Jan Kott, *Shakespeare Our Contemporary*, Methuen, 1965
An influential, but now much criticised political reading of Shakespeare's plays. Kott's chapter on *Antony and Cleopatra* claims that '*Antony and Cleopatra* is a tragedy about the smallness of the world . . . The world is small, because to master it, chance, or a helping hand, or a skilful blow will do'.

Richard Madelaine, *Shakespeare in Performance, Antony and Cleopatra*, Cambridge University Press, 1998
An excellent account of the worldwide performance history of the play from 1759 to 1995, together with detailed commentary on how actors have played the main parts.

Kenneth Parker, *Antony and Cleopatra*, Northcote House and British Council, 2000
A stimulating discussion of criticism of the play; especially good on feminist approaches.

Caroline Spurgeon, *Shakespeare's Imagery and What It Tells Us*, Cambridge University Press, 1935
Spurgeon claims that the dominant imagery of *Antony and Cleopatra* arises from 'the world, the firmament, the ocean and vastness generally'.

Derek Traversi, *An Approach to Shakespeare, 2: Troilus and Cressida to The Tempest*, 3rd edition, Hollis and Carter, 1969
Traversi's chapter on *Antony and Cleopatra* sees the play as a 'tragedy of waste and vanity'.

Films and audio books

Films
Antony and Cleopatra (USA, 1972) Director: Charlton Heston. Charlton Heston (Antony), Hildegard Neil (Cleopatra).
A Hollywood technicolour spectacular with gladiators fighting, a sea battle between the galleys of Rome and Egypt, a cavalry charge and extravagant sets and costumes.

Antony and Cleopatra (UK, 1974) Director: Jon Scofield. Richard Johnson (Antony), Janet Suzman (Cleopatra).
A television adaptation of Trevor Nunn's 1972 stage production for the Royal Shakespeare Company (with the Pompey subplot cut).

Antony and Cleopatra (UK, 1981) Director: Jonathan Miller. Colin Blakeley (Antony), Jane Lapotaire (Cleopatra).
Made for the BBC/Time-Life series of all Shakespeare's plays.

Audio books
Versions are available in the series by Naxos, Arkangel, HarperCollins and the BBC Radio Collection.

Antony and Cleopatra on the Web
If you type 'Antony and Cleopatra Shakespeare' into your search engine, it may find over 40,000 items. Because websites are of wildly varying quality, and rapidly disappear or are created, no recommendation can safely be made. But if you have time to browse, you may find much of interest.